GLOBE FEARON
HISTORICAL CASE STUDIES

THE
CIVIL RIGHTS
MOVEMENT

GLOBE FEARON
Pearson Learning Group

Julian Bond teaches courses in civil rights history and politics at the University of Virginia and the American University. He was active in the Civil Rights Movement in the early 1960s and served for twenty years in the Georgia General Assembly. He writes and speaks frequently on race-related subjects.

Stephen Middleton is Associate Professor of History at North Carolina State University. He received his Ph.D. from Miami University of Ohio. His particular field of interest is American constitutional and legal history, and their relevance to the African American experience. His books and articles deal with various aspects of race and law, including the civil rights revolution.

Rose Ann Mulford is a high school social studies teacher in the Livingston, New Jersey Public Schools. She received a Bachelor of Arts degree in elementary education at Trenton State College and a Masters degree in Educational Psychology at Montclair State University. Mrs. Mulford has completed graduate work in Constitutional Law and Government at Rutgers University. In addition to United States History, Mrs. Mulford has taught Holocaust, American Government, Psychology, and Sociology courses. Her particular field of interest is the History of Women. Mrs. Mulford wrote the first Women's Studies curriculum for Livingston High School. She is the District Affirmative Action Officer.

Editorial and Marketing Director, Secondary Supplementary: Nancy Surridge
Project Editors: Karen Bernhaut, Ann Clarkson, Lynn Kloss, Carol Schneider
Market Manager, Secondary Supplementary: Rhonda Anderson
Production Director: Kurt Scherwatzky
Production Editor: Alan Dalgleish
Electronic Page Production: Foca Company
Photo Research: Jenifer Hixson
Interior Design: Joan Jacobus
Cover Design: Joan Jacobus

ISBN 0-835-91831-9
Printed in the United States of America

7 8 9 10   07 06 05 04

Globe
Fearon

Pearson Learning Group

1-800-321-3106
www.pearsonlearning.com

CONTENTS

A single word stood for the yearnings of a people who had faced discrimination. This woman protests outside the White House in 1963.

THE CIVIL RIGHTS STRUGGLE

TERMS TO KNOW

- civil rights
- segregation
- lynching
- boycott
- sharecropper
- ghetto
- discriminate

On June 7, 1892, Homer A. Plessy took his seat in the first-class carriage of a train going from New Orleans to Covington, Louisiana. Plessy did not expect to go to Covington, however. He expected to go to jail.

Plessy was an African American. He had volunteered to challenge a Louisiana law. The law said that African Americans could not sit in the same railroad car as whites.

As Plessy sat down, a conductor came over and ordered Plessy out of the car. When Plessy refused to move, the conductor held the train at the station until a detective arrived. The detective arrested Plessy.

Plessy later stood before Judge John H. Ferguson. He told the judge that the Louisiana law that ordered the separation of the races violated the Fourteenth Amendment of the U.S. Constitution. That amendment guaranteed "the equal protection of the laws" to all U.S. citizens.

Unimpressed with his argument, Judge Ferguson found Plessy guilty of violating Louisiana law. Plessy appealed to the Louisiana Supreme Court, but it handed the case over to the U.S. Supreme Court.

In 1896, the case known as *Plessy* v. *Ferguson* reached the U.S. Supreme Court. There, seven of the nine Supreme Court justices upheld the Louisiana "separate but equal" law. They claimed that it was legal to keep the races separate as long as the state provided facilities that were "equal."

A Wall Grows

The *Plessy* decision was a huge step backward for **civil rights**. Civil rights are the rights given to U.S. citizens and protected by the Constitution. The Supreme Court's decision

gave approval to a system of **segregation,** or separation of Americans by race. The Court's ruling went far beyond separate railroad cars for African Americans and whites. It justified segregation between African Americans and whites in all types of settings.

Segregation was especially strong in the South. African Americans and whites could not ride in the same streetcars or railway cars or even sit in the same waiting areas in the stations. African Americans could not drink from the same public water fountains as whites. They had to sit in separate sections of theaters. African Americans and whites could not be treated in the same hospitals. They could not even be buried in the same cemeteries. Even though the facilities were supposed to be equal for the races, no one enforced this part of the law. The separate facilities for African Americans were rarely equal to those for whites.

This system of segregation became known as the Jim Crow laws. The name may have

Until the 1960s, a wall of segregation divided African Americans and whites. That wall existed in both the North and the South. In Cairo, Illinois, a public swimming pool suddenly became a "Private Pool," open only to "members," when African Americans tried to use it.

come from a popular song that made fun of African Americans.

Despite widespread opposition from African Americans, Jim Crow laws ruled American life for more than 50 years. From the 1950s to the 1970s, a Southern movement to win civil rights for African Americans swept through the United States.

Fighting Segregation

This book tells the story of some of the heroes of the Civil Rights Movement. It describes people who put their jobs, homes, and lives in danger by challenging segregation. Some of the people you will read about include Elizabeth Eckford, Rosa Parks, and Thurgood Marshall.

- Fifteen-year-old Elizabeth Eckford braved a cursing, threatening mob to help end segregation at Central High School in Little Rock, Arkansas.
- Tired of unfair treatment, Rosa Parks, a 42-year-old African American seamstress, refused to give up her seat on the bus to a white man.
- Thurgood Marshall, an African American lawyer, gave up a promising private practice to dedicate his life to fighting segregation in the courts.

Thousands of people—of all races—fought to win civil rights for African Americans. This book tells the story of just a few of those who inspired the Civil Rights Movement. It includes people such as Martin Luther King, Jr., Fannie Lou Hamer, Ezell Blair, Michael Schwerner, Levi Pearson, Medgar Evers, and James Meredith.

The Civil Rights Movement changed the nation. It gave new hope to African Americans. It also encouraged other minority groups to work to change their roles in U.S. society.

With all its successes, the Civil Rights Movement left many issues unresolved. African Americans and whites have not achieved equality. But the gap has narrowed.

A History of Injustice

To understand why people were willing to put their lives on the line for civil rights, it is necessary to understand how oppressive Jim Crow laws were. African Americans and whites who protested these unjust laws risked—and sometimes lost—their lives.

Thousands of African Americans were murdered in **lynchings**. To *lynch* means "to hang or otherwise murder a person by mob action without a lawful trial." Between 1882 and 1900, racist whites lynched more than 3,000 people. Most lynchings took place in the South. Almost all the victims were African Americans. This reign of terror continued well into the 1950s. The story below is just one example of the wave of lynchings that swept the South during the late 1800s.

In March 1892, 12 armed white men attacked a grocery store in Memphis, Tennessee, that was owned by three African Americans. The attackers had been encouraged by a white grocer who was angry at seeing competition from African American-owned businesses.

The three store owners, who were armed, fought back. Police arrested and jailed them, not their white attackers. As they waited for their trial, a mob of whites stormed the jail. The mob dragged the three men out into the street and murdered them.

Fighting Injustice

Ida B. Wells made it her life's work to put a stop to the lynchings of African Americans. Born into slavery in 1862, Wells became a teacher at the age of 14. She later continued her education by attending Nashville, Tennessee's Fisk University.

In 1891, Wells became the editor and part owner of a newspaper called the *Memphis Free Speech*. Wells had been a friend of Thomas Moss, one of the Memphis store owners who had been lynched. After his murder, she wrote an editorial demanding the arrest of the murderers. Nothing was done.

Perhaps the most horrible aspect of racism was the wave of lynchings that swept the United States between 1880 and the 1950s. Here, the local chapter of the NAACP pickets in front of Constitution Hall in 1934 demanding a federal law to outlaw lynching. That law would not come until the 1960s.

More of Wells's editorials only raised the anger of the city's racists. One night, a mob attacked the newspaper, destroyed the presses, and threatened to hang Wells. Wells fled the city and moved to Chicago, where she continued her fight for justice for African Americans.

Direct Action

In addition to Homer Plessy, other African Americans took direct action against Jim Crow laws. Some **boycotted** businesses that practiced segregation. To *boycott* means "to refuse to use or buy the goods or services of a company." In more than 20 Southern cities, protesters boycotted streetcar companies that segregated passengers.

The Great Migration

Beginning in 1910, large numbers of African Americans moved to the North. This movement is known as the Great Migration.

Many African Americans felt trapped in the South. Many earned their living as **sharecroppers**. A sharecropper farms a plot of land owned by another person. In exchange, the owner gives the farmer a share of the crop. In the South, the sharecropping system was designed to keep African Americans in poverty.

Sharecroppers borrowed plows, seeds, and even their houses from white landowners. They went into debt when they planted a crop. Sharecroppers usually had little money left over when they paid their debts.

African Americans who left the South wanted to find good jobs. They also hoped for a life free from segregation. They had heard that whites treated African Americans better in the North.

Faded Hopes

The North did not prove to be the paradise that many had expected. Even in the North, African Americans were closed out of many jobs and workers' unions. They were crowded into poor sections of Northern cities called **ghettos**. In the ghettos, whole families often shared one small apartment. Because of overcrowding and neglect by landlords, buildings began to fall apart. Pipes leaked, plaster fell from the ceilings, and rats scurried about.

Despite these problems, African Americans created lives for themselves in the North. They set up their own churches. Many of these churches helped new arrivals from the South. African Americans also created new businesses and community organizations. With an increasing sense of security came the spirit to change their condition.

"We Claim Every Single Right of Americans"

We claim for ourselves every single right that belongs to a free born American. . . .The battle we wage is not for ourselves alone, but for all true Americans. It is a fight for ideals, lest this [land] *become in truth the land of the thief and the home of the slave.*

The author of these stirring words was the teacher, poet, and historian, W. E. B. Du Bois. Meeting with a group of 100 African American leaders, Du Bois challenged Americans of all races to fight injustice.

In 1910, Du Bois helped form the National Association for the Advancement of Colored People, or the NAACP. The aim of the new group was to win "equal rights and opportunities for all," according to Du Bois. To achieve this goal, the NAACP brought together many of the brightest minds in the United States—both African American and white.

Over the years, the NAACP became a powerful voice for justice. After ten years, the organization had over 400 local branches and more than 91,000 members. It tried to change public opinion about discrimination. The group took out ads in newspapers. These ads described lynchings and other violence against African Americans. It also published studies on African American living conditions.

The NAACP also fought for justice in the courts. It attacked laws that **discriminated** against African Americans. To *discriminate* means "to treat someone in a different way based on his or her race, religion, or sex." Over the years, the NAACP won court victories in fair housing, education, and voting rights.

Depression and War

African Americans suffered more than most Americans during the Great Depression. They were often the first to be fired from their jobs. Because African Americans were poorer than most Americans, they had less saved to help them through the difficult times. As African American poet Langston Hughes wrote,

> *The Depression brought everyone down a peg or two. And the Negroes had but a few pegs to fall.*

However, the labor shortage created by World War II opened new opportunities for African Americans. Millions of African Americans moved from Southern farms and small towns to cities in the North, West, and Midwest. Many served in the armed forces. Others took important jobs in defense industries.

In World War II, the United States fought for freedom abroad. But it still denied some of its own citizens equal rights. African American leaders said that they wanted both a victory over enemies abroad and a victory over racism at home.

World War II ended on September 2, 1945. Whether they had been in the armed forces or at home, the war had changed the lives of African Americans. Many had worked at new jobs, gone to new places, and seen new things. For the first time, African Americans had earned a good living. After the war, some veterans took advantage of the GI Bill, which paid for their college education. African Americans faced the future with more hope and greater expectations.

World War II opened new opportunities for African Americans. These women welders helped build some of the most powerful U.S. ships in the U.S. Navy. African Americans were well aware that while the United States was fighting for freedom in Europe and Asia, it denied many American citizens their equal rights.

A New Era Dawns

On April 18, 1946, fans packed the stands of a ballpark in Jersey City, New Jersey. They had come to see the New York Giants play an exhibition game with the Montreal Royals, the top minor league team of the Brooklyn Dodgers. Why was there so much interest in a baseball game between a minor and a major league team?

People had come to see the first baseman, Jackie Robinson, play for the Royals. He was the first African American to play for a team outside the Negro National League. Robinson opened the way for other African American baseball players to play in the major leagues.

Still, Robinson knew that winning equality for African Americans took more than hitting a baseball. Remembering his boyhood in Pasadena, California, in the 1920s, he said:

We saw movies from segregated balconies, swam in the municipal pool only on Tuesdays and were permitted in the YMCA only one night a week. Restaurant doors were slammed in our faces.

Robinson soon decided to work for the Civil Rights Movement. This movement worked to extend the Constitution's promise of equality to all Americans.

Thinking It Over

1. How did the case of *Plessy* v. *Ferguson* affect African Americans' civil rights?
2. What was the Great Migration?

The myth of segregation was that schools were "separate but equal." But, as this Alabama school shows, facilities were far from equal.

JIM CROW IS EXPELLED FROM SCHOOL

CRITICAL QUESTIONS

- Can governments keep people segregated and still treat them equally?
- Does growing up in a segregated society harm young people?

TERMS TO KNOW

- psychology
- unanimous
- desegregate
- integration
- literacy
- poll tax

ACTIVE LEARNING

At the end of this case study, you will be asked to write an essay about the equality of segregated schools. An essay is a short composition that usually gives the writer's opinion on a topic. As you read this case study, take notes to describe your thoughts on the issue of segregated schools.

Clarendon County, South Carolina, in 1948 was a poor rural area with no major industries. The county had a large population of African Americans. About seven out of every ten people were African American. Two-thirds of the African American families in Clarendon County earned less than $1,000 a year.

Clarendon County was located far from the exciting changes that were taking place in the North. Jackie Robinson was in his first year with the Brooklyn Dodgers. But the local newspapers rarely covered his achievements. All sports were segregated in Clarendon County. The sports pages were filled with news of white teams.

Few people knew of leading African American actors, such as Paul Robeson, or musicians, such as Charlie Parker. African American writers, such as Langston Hughes and Zora Neale Hurston, were also almost unknown.

The people of Clarendon County lived in a highly segregated society. Movie theaters were segregated. Stores had separate entrances for the races. There were separate water fountains, churches, hospitals, and cemeteries, as well as separate school systems.

Active Learning: Take notes on these conditions and the others that you will read about in this case study. You will incorporate your findings in an essay on whether separate but equal systems were truly equal.

1 First Challenges

The African American school system was clearly inferior to the white system. All-black schools were run down. Some had no water fountains. At one school, students had to carry buckets of drinking water from a nearby home before classes started each morning.

None of the African American schools had an inside toilet. Students were forced to use an outhouse in the fields. One school did not have any desks. Students sat at a few wobbly tables.

Clarendon County spent only $43 per year to educate each African American student. It spent $179 for each white student. The system bought new books for the white schools, but it never bought new books for the African American schools. African American students were given "new" books only after the white students were finished with them.

White students spent the full school year, from September to June, in school. Most African American students spent only about six months in school. They were often taken

Grinding poverty forced African American children in the South into back-breaking labor in the steamy cotton fields.

out of school to help with the planting and harvesting of crops.

Mirror on the Country

Clarendon County, South Carolina, mirrored conditions that occurred all over the Deep South. In 1949, the state of Alabama spent $108 a year on every white student, but only $30 on every African American student. In Arkansas, 23 percent of the students were African American. However, the state spent only 12 percent of its funds to pay for the African American students' education.

Since the time of slavery, many African Americans have believed that education is crucial to breaking down discrimination. Through education, people could get better jobs, enter professions, and overcome housing barriers.

Long after the Civil War, white and African American students still attended segregated schools. In 1896, the Supreme Court approved segregated schools in the case of *Plessy* v. *Ferguson*. The Court ruled that separate school systems were legal as long as they were equal. In the real world, separate schools were not equal.

Standing Up for What Is Right

Not everyone in Clarendon County was prepared to accept the segregated school system. One person who stood up for what he knew was right was a poor African American farmer named Levi Pearson.

Pearson had grown cotton in the rich brown soil of Clarendon County all his life. As his three children grew up, Pearson saw how the segregated schools doomed them to a life of poverty.

White children had nine new buses to take them to school. African American children had to find their own way to school. So early every morning before he went out to work in the fields, Pearson drove his three children nine miles to their run-down school.

When African American parents asked for a new bus, the superintendent said no. He claimed that the county just did not have the money. So the parents bought a second-hand bus to carry their children to school.

Then they asked the superintendent if the county would provide gasoline for the bus. Again, he said no, and claimed that the county did not have the money.

In 1947, Pearson and several other African American parents sued the school board. Soon after the lawsuit began, Pearson ran into trouble. Every white-owned store in the county cut off his credit. He could not buy supplies for his farm. He could not get loans from banks.

To earn money for fertilizer, he cut and sold timber. But when the owner of the lumber mill found out who Pearson was, he refused to pick up the logs that Pearson had cut.

In 1948, a court threw out Pearson's case. That summer, Levi Pearson could not get any white farmer with a harvester to help him bring in his crop. He had to sit and watch his oats, beans, and wheat rot in the fields.

Pearson would not give up, though. In March 1949, he and a small group of farmers traveled to South Carolina's state capital. In Columbia, the farmers met Thurgood Marshall, an African American lawyer. Marshall worked for the National Association for the Advancement of Colored People (NAACP).

Levi Pearson told Marshall about the injustices African American children experienced in Clarendon County. At first, Marshall said nothing. At the end of the meeting, he gave the group a challenge: We must fight this battle together. He said that they needed to find 20 people who were willing to sue the county, and not just for buses. He also told them that they must ask for equal treatment in everything, including buses, buildings, teachers' salaries, and teaching materials. Everything should be equal for African Americans and whites.

A Life for Justice

Who was Thurgood Marshall—the man who gave this advice? At the time of the meeting, Marshall was the chief lawyer for the NAACP. Over the years, Marshall had tackled the issue of school segregation with great courage. He had a reputation as the African American lawyer who "stood up in white men's courts."

A Good Book to Read

Fight for Freedom: The Story of the NAACP, by Langston Hughes. NY: W.W. Norton, 1962.

The famous African American poet, whose work defined the African American experience, also wrote this moving history in which he was a participant.

Just becoming a lawyer had been an accomplishment for Marshall. He was born in Baltimore in 1908. His father was a railroad dining-car waiter. His mother was a teacher at a segregated elementary school. As a child, Marshall's family encouraged him to work for what he knew to be right.

As a teenager, Marshall took a summer job as a waiter on the railroad. On his first day of work, his manager gave Marshall a uniform that was far too small. Marshall asked for a larger uniform. His manager refused his request, saying:

> Boy, we can get a shorter Negro to fit these pants a lot easier than we can get new pants to fit you.

Needing the job to continue his education, Marshall said nothing.

Active Learning: What might you do if an employer said the same thing to you? Why do you think Thurgood Marshall responded as he did? Note your responses and keep them for your essay.

Marshall worked his way through college. Then he earned his law degree from Howard University. He entered into private practice for a brief time. Later, Marshall practiced under Charles H. Houston, a Harvard law school graduate and legal director for the NAACP. Then, in 1938, Marshall was named chief counsel for the NAACP.

Marshall had a great deal of work to do in his battle against discrimination. A number of his early cases saved the lives of African Americans who had been sentenced to death on murder charges. These charges were often invented to punish people for their work for civil rights.

Once Marshall disguised himself as a sharecropper to investigate a lynching on a farm in Mississippi. If Marshall's real identity had been discovered, he could have been lynched himself. More and more, Marshall came to see that the key to winning justice for African Americans in the South was winning the right to equal education.

The battle for equal education would be very difficult. There were more than 11,000 segregated school districts. The NAACP did not have a large enough staff to sue every school district. So it decided to focus on a few cases and try to get these cases to the Supreme Court.

All-Out Attack

In June 1950, Marshall held a meeting of top NAACP lawyers. The purpose of the meeting was to map out an all-out attack on segregation in elementary and secondary schools. In the early 1950s, tackling segregated schooling was a huge goal. Twenty-one states, as well as Washington, D.C., had segregated schools. However, Marshall told his team of lawyers:

> We are going to insist on no segregation in American public education from top to bottom—from law school to kindergarten.

Linda Brown tried to enter an all-white school in Topeka, Kansas. From this attempt, came the case that shook American education to its roots.

Thinking It Over

1. What were some of the differences between the all-white and all-African American schools in Clarendon County?
2. What risks did African Americans face in challenging the system of segregation in the Deep South?

2 The *Brown* Case

In 1950, eight-year-old Linda Brown attended Monroe Elementary School in Topeka, Kansas. To get to school, Brown and her two sisters had to walk six blocks. They then crossed busy railroad tracks and waited for a rickety old bus to take them to school.

One morning, in September 1950, just before the new school year began, Reverend Oliver Brown took his daughter for a walk. They walked six blocks and found themselves in front of the attractive Sumner School, which was a school for white students. As they climbed the school's stairs, Brown could feel the tension in her father's manner.

They were directed to the principal's office. Brown waited outside while her father went in to see the principal. When he came out, he was very upset. The principal had told him that his daughter could not go to the Sumner School because it was for whites only.

Reverend Brown decided to sue the city to win his daughter's right to attend the neighborhood school. Reverend Brown had often discussed the evils of school segregation with his friends. He found that seven other African Americans were willing to join him in suing the Topeka Board of Education. Because Brown was first in alphabetical order, the family's name was given to the case.

An Important Difference

Previous cases had focused on the differences in quality between African American schools and white schools. Reverend Brown and other Topeka parents said that conditions in the schools did not matter all that much. The very existence of segregated schools was the issue. African American parents argued that their children could not get an equal education in segregated schools. It did not matter how new the books, how sparkling the gyms, or how small the classes were.

"I and My Children are Craving Light"

The *Brown* case made its way through the Kansas court system. During one hearing, the judge allowed Silas Fleming, an African American parent, to explain why it was important to end segregation in education.

> SILAS FLEMING: I would ask for a few minutes to explain why I got into the [lawsuit], body and soul.
>
> JUDGE: All right, go ahead and tell it.
>
> SILAS FLEMING: Well,...it wasn't to suggest that our teachers are not capable of teaching our children, because they are supreme, extremely intelligent, and are capable of teaching my kids or white or any kids. But my point was that not only I and my children are craving light. The entire colored race is craving light. And the only way to reach the light is to start our children together in their infancy and they come up together.

The "Doll Doctor" and Segregation

Thurgood Marshall was one of the lawyers for the *Brown* case. One of Marshall's strongest arguments had nothing to do with law. It dealt with **psychology**. Psychology is the study of the human mind and behavior. In particular, Marshall turned his attention to the way segregation affected the self-esteem of African American children.

To demonstrate segregation's effects on children, Marshall called on Dr. Kenneth Clark. Dr. Clark was the first African American professor at the City College of New York. Dr. Clark and his wife, Mamie Phipps Clark, had conducted many experiments with African

Does growing up in a segregated school harm a child? Professor Kenneth Clark studied school segregation. He was able to prove how deeply segregation wounded African American children.

GOING TO THE SOURCE

The "Doll Doctor" and Segregation

Some of the most important testimony during the *Brown* case had nothing to do with law. Dr. Kenneth Clark and his wife studied the psychological impact of segregation on African American children. The most important test involved using two sets of dolls, one colored pink, the other colored brown. The "doll tests" provided strong evidence of the destructive force of school segregation.

JUDGE: Now, Professor Clark, you had occasion, did you not, to test the reactions of children involved in this case to determine sensitivity to racial segregation.

PROFESSOR CLARK: Yes I did.

JUDGE: Now, will you tell us what you did.

PROFESSOR CLARK: I used these methods which I told you about—the Negro and White dolls—which were identical in every respect except skin color. I presented these dolls to them, and I asked them the following questions in the following order:

'Show me the doll that you like best or that you'd like to play with. Show me the nice doll. Show me the doll that looks bad. Give me the doll that looks like you.'

JUDGE: Like you?

PROFESSOR CLARK: Like you. I wanted to get the child's free expression of his opinions before I had him identify with one of these two dolls.

I found that 10 of the 16 children between the ages of six and nine whom I tested chose the white doll as their preference. Eleven of the children chose the brown doll as the doll which looked 'bad.'...

My opinion is that a fundamental effect of segregation is basic confusion in the individuals and their concepts about themselves....This is an example of how the pressures which these children sensed against being brown forced them to evade reality—to escape the reality which seems too burdening or threatening.... These children in Clarendon County, like other human beings who are subjected to an inferior status, have been definitely harmed, that the signs of instability are clear.

From *Removing a Badge of Slavery: The Record of Brown v. Board of Education,* ed. Mark Whitman. NY: Markus Wiener Publishing Company, 1993 pp. 49–51.

1. What were Professor Clark's methods in interviewing the children?
2. What judgments did Professor Clark make about the impact of school segregation on African American students?

American children. Their goal was to measure the impact of segregation on children.

The Clarks had tested African American children's views of themselves by using four dolls. The dolls were identical in every way except one. Two of the dolls had pink skin and two had brown skin. (See "Going to the Source" on page 17 for details.)

At the trial, Dr. Clark and other psychologists showed that segregation made African American children regard themselves as inferior to whites. Thus, Marshall argued, the practice of school segregation violated the Fourteenth Amendment. That amendment promised "the equal protection of the laws" to all citizens.

Defenders of Segregated Schools

The supporters of segregation mounted a powerful case. They argued that the Constitution did not give the federal government the power to run schools. In other words, the federal government could not interfere in local issues. If states wanted to keep their school systems segregated, that was their right.

Furthermore, the defenders of segregation argued that this policy was good for students. They said that local governments were better able than national government to determine what type of education parents wanted. As one lawyer representing South Carolina stated:

> Surely the Supreme Court does not want to sit as a glorified Board of Education for the state of South Carolina.

Short-Changing African American Students

Thurgood Marshall, however, argued more powerfully against segregation. He showed just how harmful segregation was to African American students. It didn't matter if African American schools were poorer than all-white schools or if they had just as much money. Marshall argued that even if the money were equal, segregation by itself short-changed African American students. "Separate but equal" schools could never be truly equal.

Thinking It Over

1. Why did Reverend Brown want to enroll his daugther in an all white School?
2. What was the contribution of Dr. Kenneth Clark in the *Brown* case?

3 "'Separate But Equal' Has No Place"

On May 17, 1954, before packed chambers of the U.S. Supreme Court, Chief Justice Earl Warren read the Court's decision:

> To separate [the African American children] from others of similar age and qualifications solely because of their race generates a feeling of inferiority....We conclude that in the field of public education the doctrine of "separate but equal" has no place. Separate educational facilities are...unequal.

It was a **unanimous** decision. All nine justices agreed. Four of these justices were white Southerners. This ruling ended more than half a century of government support for segregated schools.

Resisting Desegregation

The Supreme Court ruled that African Americans must be allowed to attend the same schools as white students. Chief Justice Warren said that the results of Professor Clark's doll test were important in making his decision.

The Court ordered school districts to **desegregate,** or end, segregation. Many did. Within a year after the 1954 decision, more than 500 school districts in the North and upper South ended segregation. In Baltimore, Maryland, and Washington, D.C., African Americans and whites sat side-by-side for the first time in school. But many districts did not desegregate.

Brown II

A year later, Thurgood Marshall returned to the Supreme Court. The Court wanted to make sure that schools obeyed the *Brown* ruling. In a decision known as *Brown* II, the Court issued guidelines that placed the responsibility for desegregation on local school officials. The

On the steps of the U.S. Supreme Court, Thurgood Marshall celebrates the historic ruling outlawing school segregation with NAACP lawyers George Hayes and James Nabrit.

Court ordered school districts to begin desegregation "with all deliberate speed."

What did this phrase mean? No one was sure. To African American parents, "deliberate speed" might mean in a few months. To Southern racists, "deliberate speed" might mean 25 years—or never.

After *Brown* II, hopes for a quick end to segregation faded. Stiff resistance to desegregation quickly developed in the Deep South. The day after the *Brown* decision, reporters interviewed a number of white Southern leaders. What they said was not comforting to those who supported **integration**. To integrate means "to bring together." Senator James O. Eastland of Mississippi said, "We will take whatever steps are necessary to retain segregation in education." Other leaders echoed his remarks. It would be many years before legal segregation in the South ended.

"We Haven't Begun to Work Yet"

On the evening after the Court's ruling on *Brown*, members of the NAACP team celebrated. Marshall was subdued. "You guys go ahead and have your fun. But remember, we haven't begun to work yet."

He was right. The civil rights struggle was just beginning. How far would white Southern leaders go to resist segregation? The answer would come in Little Rock, Arkansas, in 1957, when nine African Americans registered for the all-white Central High School. (See Case Study 2.)

A Member of the Court

For Thurgood Marshall, winning the *Brown* case capped a brilliant career with the NAACP. Then in 1961, President John F. Kennedy named Marshall a judge on the U.S. Court of Appeals. This court hears cases that have been decided in lower courts, but whose decisions

A new age in American society was dawning in May 1954, but few could tell exactly where it would lead. The day after the Supreme Court ruling, Mrs. Nettie Hunt, sitting on the steps of the Court building, explains some of the opportunities that her daughter will have that were closed to Mrs. Hunt.

are being appealed, or challenged, by one of the sides.

In 1967, Thurgood Marshall became the first African American to be appointed to the Supreme Court. In announcing his appointment, President Lyndon Johnson said:

> *I believe that Thurgood Marshall has already earned his place in history, but I think it will be greatly advanced by his service on the Court....I believe it is the right thing to do, the right time to do it, the right man, and the right place.*

As a justice of the Supreme Court, Thurgood Marshall fought hard for the rights of privacy and free speech and against unfair treatment by law enforcement. He spoke out strongly against the death penalty. He also argued against discrimination because of race or gender. When he retired in 1991, Marshall asked to be remembered as someone who "did the best he could with what he had."

Thinking It Over

1. How did the Supreme Court rule in the case of *Brown* v. *Topeka Board of Education*?
2. (a) What was the ruling in *Brown II*? (b) Why were African Americans in the South worried about the decision in *Brown II*?

Case Study Review

Identifying Main Ideas

1. Why did Levi Pearson sue the school system of Clarendon County?

2. Why did Oliver Brown sue the Topeka, Kansas, school district?

3. What problems arose from the Supreme Court's order to begin school desegregation "with all deliberate speed?"

Working Together

Form a small group. Create posters to advertise public meetings on the Supreme Court's ruling in each of the following cases: *Plessy* v. *Ferguson*, *Brown* v. *Topeka Board of Education*, and *Brown* II. Your posters should outline the key issues of each case and explain why it is important to discuss these cases at a public meeting.

Active Learning

Writing a Persuasive Essay Review the notes you took as you read the case study. Create a persuasive essay on segregated schools. Your essay does not need to contain all the details covered in this case study. However, it should give your readers a strong sense of your opinion about segregated schools. Give your first draft to a classmate to review. Then review the essay yourself. Finally, revise it and prepare a final copy.

Lessons for Today

Today, more than 40 years after the *Brown* case, unequal schools still exist. Wealthy communities spend far more on their schools than do poor communities. Is this difference fair? Should there be equal funding of schools? Or should each community be allowed to determine how much money it will spend for its schools?

What Might You Have Done?

Imagine you are a poor African American sharecropper in Clarendon County, South Carolina, in 1947. Another farmer, Levi Pearson, approaches you with a plan to sue the county because African American students do not have buses to take them to school. You know you can be thrown off the land that you farm if the white landowner knows about your involvement with this case. What might you do?

Jim Crow and Voting Rights

Jim Crow laws did more than force African Americans to live a segregated life. Jim Crow laws also kept African Americans from voting. In some states, whites made **literacy**, or the ability to read and write, a requirement for voting. Literacy tests were given, but African Americans often didn't pass even if they could read. Officials often passed whites who could not read or write. Other states required that a person pay a tax, called a **poll tax**, in order to vote. These laws kept African Americans, who were largely poor, from voting.

Critical thinkers do not just watch the world go by. They think about whether an action or policy is right or wrong, fair or unfair, and why. They consider the reasons for an action and its consequences to help them make up their minds. You may have already decided that Jim Crow laws were wrong. But what made them wrong? Answer the questions below to help you find out.

1. How was the 'separate but equal' policy supposed to work?

2. How did the 'separate but equal' policy really work?

Under Jim Crow laws, African Americans and whites lived in different worlds. Use the diagram below to evaluate what effects these laws had on society. The circle in the center represents the groups divided by Jim Crow laws. The boxes represent some of its effects. Copy the diagram into your notebook. In the boxes, fill in the facts and details that describe these effects.

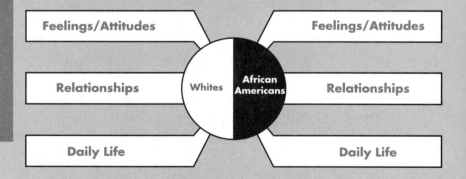

3. Suppose the 'separate but equal' principle had been strictly followed. Would a genuinely 'separate but equal' system be fair? Would you be in favor of it? Why or why not? Give reasons for your answers.

African American students ignore jeering crowds and reporters as they try to enter Little Rock's Central High School in 1957.

THE MOB AT CENTRAL HIGH SCHOOL

CRITICAL QUESTIONS

- Why were African Americans willing to risk their safety and their lives to integrate Southern schools?
- Why did the governor of Arkansas oppose the integration of schools so intensely?

TERMS TO KNOW

- manifesto
- federalize
- propaganda

ACTIVE LEARNING

After you read this case study, you will be asked to write a newspaper article on the events that took place at Central High School in 1957. As you read the story, take notes to help you write that article. Remember, good newspaper articles answer each of the "Five Ws": *Who, What, When, Where,* and *Why.*

Starting a new school is never easy. However, few students have had to live through what happened to 15-year-old Elizabeth Eckford on September 4, 1957, in Little Rock, Arkansas.

The first scene Eckford saw when she got off the bus a block from Central High School was a sea of angry faces. She tried to walk to the school, but a jeering mob blocked her path. All alone, her knees shaking, she pushed through the mob. She was trying hard not to show her fright. "It was the longest block I ever walked in my whole life," she said later.

Eckford was one of nine students who had volunteered to be among the first African Americans to attend Central High School.

When she left for school that morning, Eckford thought there might be trouble. But she didn't know that she would see hundreds of angry white people who had been waiting for her since early morning. Suddenly a shout went through the crowd. Elizabeth Eckford was attempting to enter the school.

No Help from the Guard

As Eckford approached the school, she saw the mob surging towards her. People in the mob cursed at her.

Soldiers armed with rifles and bayonets lined the entrance to the school. Eckford thought, "Stay calm. At least if I reach the soldiers, I'll be safe."

Eckford was wrong. At the main entrance, soldiers blocked the door. She went down the line of soldiers, but no one would give way. She found a side door, but a soldier raised his bayonet to keep her from entering.

Eckford did not know what to do. She decided to go home. As she headed toward the bus stop, about 50 angry whites surrounded her. They cursed and spat at her. "Lynch her! Lynch her!" "Find a tree for the nigger."

Eckford tried to find a friendly face in the mob. She saw an elderly white woman and asked her for help. The woman looked at her calmly and spat at her.

Eckford turned back to the guards, but they did nothing. She walked back to the bus stop and sat down at the bench. Again, the mob surrounded her. "Get a rope. Drag her over to this tree! Let's take care of the nigger."

A white woman fought her way through the mob, screaming, "Leave this child alone. Why are you tormenting her? Six months from now, you will hang your heads in shame."

The woman, Grace Lorch, sat down with Eckford on the bench. She put her arm around the girl and stayed there until the bus arrived. Mrs. Lorch rode with Eckford until she got off at the school where her mother taught.

"Mother was standing at the window with her head bowed," Eckford later recalled. "She must have sensed I was there because she turned around. She looked as if she had been crying, and I wanted to tell her I was all right. But I couldn't speak. She put her arms around me and I cried."

1 "Stone This Time. Dynamite Next!"

About one month before Elizabeth Eckford tried to enter Central High, Daisy Bates was reading a newspaper in her living room. Suddenly, a rock crashed through her window.

Covered with shards of glass, Bates reached for the stone. A note was tied to it. Scrawled in childish print was a threat:

"Stone This Time. Dynamite Next!"

Suddenly, Bates knew that this was the beginning of a war. As the president of the Arkansas state NAACP, she had fought hard to make the Arkansas school board integrate Central High. In this case, the integration involved bringing together African American and white students. Bates realized then that she was risking her safety and the safety of her family to support integration at Central High.

Braving the fury of the mob, Elizabeth Eckford makes her way toward the school. Later, she said, "The crowd moved in closer and then began to follow me, called me names...My knees started to shake and all of a sudden I wondered whether I could make it...."

Resistance in the Deep South

The rock thrown through Daisy Bates's window was the latest blow in the war that had begun after the Supreme Court's ruling in *Brown* v. *Board of Education*. (See Case Study 1.)

The Supreme Court had ordered all school districts in the U.S. to desegregate "with all deliberate speed."

Many school districts obeyed the Court's order. But there was widespread resistance in the South. Many Americans expected southern school boards and governors to act in good faith in setting their own deadlines for desegregation. To many white Southerners, however, the deadline was "never."

White Citizens' Councils were formed throughout the South. These groups promised to oppose integration in every community. The

Ku Klux Klan became more active and used terror and violence to silence those who said the South should accept the *Brown* decision.

The rise of these hate groups changed the political climate. In 1954, Arkansas Governor Francis Cherry said of the *Brown* ruling: "Arkansas will obey the law."

Six months later, the climate was different. Arkansas was in the midst of an election campaign for governor. Candidate Orval Faubus, who later won the election, made it clear that integration would be the issue in the campaign. He said:

Arkansas is not ready for a complete mixing of the races. Any attempt to solve this problem by pressure will hurt the good relations which exist between whites and Negroes. I am making my position clear to discourage those who might seek to play upon

racial prejudice for selfish ends or, as in the case of communism, to create ill will between whites and Negroes.

A Communist Plot?

Faubus used arguments to oppose civil rights that would become familiar in the years ahead. He claimed that there were good relations between African Americans and whites in the South. It was "outside agitators" that were spoiling these good relations. Many of those supporting integration were communists or communist supporters. He said that African Americans themselves did not want integration.

In March 1956, 96 Southern congressmen issued a Southern Manifesto. A **manifesto** is a statement of beliefs. The Southern Manifesto expressed these congressmen's opposition to the *Brown* ruling. It called for "all lawful means to bring about a reversal of this decision which is against the Constitution."

Schools were set to open on September 3, 1957, in Little Rock, Arkansas. A Federal court ordered Central High to admit nine African American pupils. The city's school board then prepared a plan to obey the *Brown* decision.

Active Learning: Make note of Faubus's comments on desegregation. Be sure to respond to his arguments in your newspaper article.

As the date for the opening of schools approached, tensions rose. Racists made threats that "blood will flow in the streets" if desegregation continued. In August, a local judge threw out the original integration ruling. Then a few days later, a federal judge

After the Brown ruling, a federal court ordered Central High School to admit nine African American students. Here are the Little Rock Nine—as these students were called.

overturned the local judge's ruling and ordered Central High to integrate.

Meanwhile, hate campaigns rose to an even higher level. Several speakers from the Mississippi and Louisiana Klans appeared in Little Rock. They threatened "bloodshed if necessary" to keep schools segregated. Rumors spread that the Klan was organizing for a fight to the finish against integrated schools. Central High School would be the first battleground.

The Governor Steps In

The night before the nine African American students walked through the doors of Central High, Governor Faubus acted. He announced that he was sending the Arkansas National Guard to the school. According to Faubus, the city needed the troops "to preserve order."

All Faubus really wanted to preserve was segregation. Faubus said that he would not permit any African American students to enter Central High. He warned that "blood will run in the streets" if they tried to enter.

Faubus was not trying to maintain order or uphold the law. Instead, his wild words were aimed at encouraging those who wanted to use violence to oppose integration.

On September 4, 1957, the stage was set for conflict at Central High School. On one side were the forces of violence and racism. On the other were nine African American students.

Thinking It Over

1. What was the attitude of the White Citizens' Councils toward the proposed integration of Central High School?
2. Who was Governor Orval Faubus really referring to when he used the term "communist supporters"?

The students were Elizabeth Eckford, Thelma Mothershed, Minnijean Brown, Gloria Ray, Ernest Green, Terrance Roberts, Carlotta Walls, Jefferson Thomas, and Melba Pattillo.

2 Carrying the Banner

On December 7, 1941, Melba Pattillo was born in Little Rock, Arkansas. A few days later, she developed a massive infection. Her temperature soared to 106° F, and she started convulsing. Her parents rushed her to the nearest hospital—one that treated only whites.

The staff reluctantly admitted the baby. She lay on the edge of death for days. When nurses would not care for her, the baby's mother and grandmother took turns treating her infection. Two days later, the baby began to improve.

Fifteen years later, Melba Pattillo was selected with eight other African Americans to integrate Little Rock's Central High School. That day, Pattillo's grandmother told her, "Now you see, that's the reason God spared your life. You're supposed to carry this banner for our people."

"I'm Coming Over to Bomb You"

September 2, 1957 was Labor Day. Melba Pattillo and her family shared one last picnic of the summer. She heard rumors from her aunt that Governor Faubus was going to prevent the African American students' entry by sending in the National Guard.

That evening, the Pattillo family turned on the television to hear Governor Faubus speak. Melba Pattillo listened as Faubus announced that he was sending troops to Central High School. Then Faubus said something that Pattillo remembered, which "made chills creep up and down my spine."

After his classes at Central High School, Jefferson Thomas stands alone on a corner waiting for a ride. White students scream threats and curses at him. Why do you think the Little Rock Nine were willing to risk their lives to integrate the all-white school?

I must state here in all sincerity that I believe that it will not be possible to restore or maintain order and protect the lives and property of the citizens if forcible integration is carried out tomorrow.

Later that night, the phone rang. A gruff voice said that he knew the Pattillo address and that he was coming to bomb the house. The family's grandmother stayed up the entire night to guard the house.

Melba Pattillo could hardly sleep that night. She tossed and turned, wondering if the risk to herself and her family was worth the effort to attend Central High School.

Day of Reckoning

Pattillo awoke on the morning of September 4, 1957 to hear a radio announcing:

Hundreds of Little Rock citizens are gathered in front of Central High School awaiting the arrival of the Negro children. We are told people have come from as far away as Mississippi, Louisiana, and Georgia to join forces to halt integration.

At 7:55 A.M., Pattillo could see a mass of white people in the street in front of Central High. At first she couldn't see what was happening. All she could hear were the cries and insults.

"Niggers go home!"

"Two, four, six, eight, we ain't gonna integrate."

Then she saw Elizabeth Eckford trying to get into the school. When the mob saw Pattillo, it rushed toward her. One man grabbed her arm, but she pulled away. Then Pattillo's mother pushed her toward their car, but part of

GOING TO THE SOURCE

Elizabeth Eckford's First Day at Central High School

Elizabeth Eckford was one of the nine African American students who integrated Central High School in 1957. Because of a mix-up, she faced the full anger of the mob alone. Below is her account of what happened on that first day of school.

Before I left home, Mother called us into the living room. She said we should have a word of prayer. Then I caught the bus and I got off a block from the school. I saw a large crowd of people standing across the street from the soldiers guarding Central. As I walked on, the crowd suddenly got very quiet....I looked at all the people and thought, "Maybe I will be safer if I walk down the block to the front entrance behind the guards."

At the corner I tried to pass through the long line of guards around the school so as to enter the grounds behind them. One of the guards pointed across the street. So I pointed in the same direction and asked whether he meant for me to cross the street and walk down. He nodded "yes." So, I walked across the street conscious of the crowd that stood there, but they moved away from me.

For a moment all I could hear was the shuffling of their feet. Then someone shouted, "Here she comes, get ready!" I moved away from the crowd on the sidewalk and into the street. If the mob came at me, I could then cross back over so the guards could protect me.

The crowd moved in closer and then began to follow me, called me names. I still wasn't afraid. Just a little bit nervous. Then my knees started to shake and all of a sudden I wondered whether I could make it to the center entrance a block away. It was the longest block I ever walked in my whole life.

Even so, I still wasn't too scared because all the time I kept thinking that the guards would protect me....

The crowd was quiet. I guess they were waiting to see what was going to happen. When I was able to steady my knees, I walked up to the guard who had let the white students in. He too didn't move. When I tried to squeeze past him, he raised his bayonet and then the other guards closed in and they raised their bayonets.

From *The Long Shadow of Little Rock,* by Daisy Bates
NY: *David McKay, 1962), pp. 73–76.*

1. What was Eckford's first thought when she got off the bus and saw the mob waiting for her?
2. Why do you suppose Eckford, who was calm at first, suddenly got so nervous that her "knees started to shake"?

the crowd came after her. "They're getting away." One man swung a tree limb at her, but just missed. Another grabbed at her mother.

Pattillo and her mother barely reached their car. Men pounded on the windshield; another threw a brick that just missed the car. Although Pattillo had just received her driver's license, she managed to steer the car through the mob and along back streets toward home.

When she got home, she learned that the other African American students had also been turned away at the school's entrance.

Active Learning: For your article, make notes about Pattillo's experience. Include in your notes words that describe the behavior of the crowd and the way Patillo must have felt.

In the Depths of Despair

Behind the locked windows of the high school, white students and administrators watched these events with different feelings. Elizabeth Huckaby was the girls' vice president at Central High. For months, she had worked quietly to make sure that the school would integrate peacefully. She went

Thinking It Over

1. What was the attitude of the National Guard troops at the entrance to Central High School? Why did they act this way?
2. If you could ask Melba Pattillo one question about her experiences during September 1957, what would it be?

to school that morning with a sense of excitement. She thought that she had finally achieved her goal.

That afternoon, Huckaby went home saddened and defeated. She watched the television news and scanned the newspapers. That night, she wrote in her journal: "Read the awful stories. Saw the awful pictures—the dignity of the rejected Negro girl, the obscenity of the faces of her tormentors."

3 Mob Rule

The next day, Little Rock newspapers ran banner headlines:

"RING OF TROOPS BLOCKS INTEGRATION HERE"

"ARMED TROOPS TURN BACK 9 NEGROES AT CENTRAL HIGH"

Photographers had also captured the events of the previous day. As the jeering crowd followed Elizabeth Eckford back to the bus stop, one photographer shot photos of her bravely—and seemingly calmly—passing through the racist mob. One picture was published in newspapers around the world. People were shocked to see the whites' blind, raw hatred. The name "Little Rock" became associated with mob rule and violence.

The Mob Goes Wild

On Friday, September 20, 1957, a federal court held a hearing on Governor Faubus's actions. In the middle of the hearing, the governor's lawyers walked out.

Early Monday morning, the nine students slipped past the mob and entered Central High by a side door. When the mob learned that the nine students were in the school, they went wild. They rushed police barricades. Unable to drag the students out of the school, the mob turned their anger on reporters and photographers. The mob beat them with fists, rocks, and sticks.

The violence spread beyond the school. Two African American women were pulled from their car and beaten. Two African American men were pulled from a truck and beaten. The windows of the truck were smashed. Later that night, the police stopped a convoy of about 100 cars. The police found dynamite, pistols, and clubs in the cars.

With the mob in control of the city, the mayor of Little Rock sent a telegram to President Dwight D. Eisenhower asking for help. For weeks now, people from around the United States had been calling for the federal government to stop mob rule in Little Rock. But only one person could give the order.

Eisenhower was angry at the way mob rule had taken over Little Rock. But he also did not want to use the power of the federal government to force racists to obey the law. He once said, "I do not believe you can change the hearts of men with laws and decisions." He just stated that, as Chief Executive of the United States, he had to enforce the Constitution.

The events in Little Rock forced Eisenhower to act. The daily newspapers showed how the mob had taken over the streets outside the high school. The mob was openly defying the courts. Governor Faubus, who should have stepped in to end mob rule, was doing nothing.

On September 24, Eisenhower finally took action. He **federalized**, or took control, of the Arkansas National Guard. He also ordered 1,000 soldiers from the combat-ready 101st Airborne Division into Little Rock. Their assignment: enforce the law and protect the nine African American students.

Grim-faced troops form a protective wall around the African American students. One soldier was assigned to each student. The soldiers walked the students to every class.

Protecting the Students

African American and white paratroopers began streaming into Little Rock early the next morning. Planes filled the sky. Immediately, the mood of the city lightened.

Two days later, the nine African American students again entered Central High. This time they were protected by the U.S. Army. As they entered the school, Minnijean Brown said to another student, "For the first time in my life, I feel like an American citizen."

Paratroopers guarded the entrances to the school. Others were stationed in the hallways. Every morning, soldiers escorted each of the African American students into the school.

A few white students took an active role in making integration work. When some white students called for a walkout to protest integration, fewer than 60 of the 1,800 students left school. A few of the white students braved rejection by sitting with the African American students at lunch. Others invited them to join the glee club. But, for the most part, the white student body never accepted the African Americans.

Many Central High teachers tried to work against racism. Elizabeth Huckaby approached the white student whom a photographer caught screaming at Elizabeth Eckford. Huckaby tried to explain that hatred destroys the people who hate. The girl just shrugged.

The Violence Resumes

The first days after the integration of Central High School went quietly. With soldiers in the halls and at the doors, the violence slowed. But after a month national guardsmen replaced U.S. soldiers. Then the harassment inside the school really began. The guardsmen themselves did not commit violence. However racist students quickly noticed that the guardsmen would look the other way when African American students were attacked.

"It Will Be Worse Tomorrow."

Two of the nine African Americans were Jefferson Thomas and Terrence Roberts. One day, Thomas and Roberts were attacked in a stairwell. Two days later, a boy hit Roberts. Several days later, a student attacked Thomas from behind and knocked him unconscious. The boy who attacked him was suspended for only three days. Thomas thought seriously about staying out of school but changed his mind. "If I stay out today, it will be worse tomorrow," he told his mother.

Although Central High was integrated, the struggle was not over. In February 1958, the Little Rock school board asked a federal judge to suspend desegregation for about two years. The judge agreed, but the Supreme Court stepped in and overturned the judge's ruling. The Court ruled that violence, or the threat of violence, could not be used to delay desegregation.

Governor Faubus then closed the high schools. He claimed the action was necessary to prevent "violence and disorder." The schools remained closed during the 1958–9 academic year. The state set up "private" academies and blocked African Americans from entering them.

Eventually, however, the courts forced the schools to reopen. When they did, token numbers of African Americans were allowed into other Little Rock schools.

Desegregation came slowly in the South. In 1957, Congress passed a new Civil Rights Act. It increased the power of the U.S. attorney general to protect African Americans' rights. But it became clear that more than court decisions were needed to end segregation. A new plan of action soon emerged in Montgomery, Alabama. (See Case Study 3.)

Cracking the Wall

In May 1958, Ernest Green was about to become the first African American to graduate from Central High. Like the other African American students, Green had faced threats all year.

Some of the Little Rock Nine pose on the steps of the Supreme Court building with Thurgood Marshall. Marshall was the NAACP's chief lawyer for Brown v. Board of Ed.

Before the graduation ceremony, Melba Pattillo confided in her diary:

Dear God,

Please walk with Ernie in the graduation line at Central. Let him be safe.

On May 27, 1957, Green received his diploma. The audience of 4,500 applauded as each of the students went on stage to receive his or her diploma. When Green appeared on stage, the audience fell silent.

Later, Green said, "I knew that once I received that diploma, I had cracked the wall…. I had accomplished what I had come there for."

Thinking It Over

1. What convinced President Eisenhower to send federal troops to Little Rock?
2. How do you think the arrival of U.S. paratroopers in Little Rock was a symbol of how the times were changing?

Case Study Review

Identifying Main Ideas

1. Why do you think the Arkansas National Guardsmen refused to help the African American students to enter Little Rock Central High School?
2. Why was Daisy Bates threatened with violence?
3. Why did the violence pick up again in the months after the African American students entered the school?

Working Together

Form a small group. Write newspaper headlines about the key events discussed in this chapter. Make a bulletin board display of your headlines.

Active Learning

Writing an Article Review the notes you took as you read this case study. Create an outline for a newspaper article about the integration of Central High School. Remember, your article does not have to contain all the details covered in this case study. However, it should give your readers the main ideas and highlights of the event. Write a first draft of your article. After you read your first draft, revise it and prepare a final copy.

Lessons for Today

The nine African American students who integrated Central High School took a stand that was both unpopular and dangerous. They had the courage to brave a dangerous mob to do what they believed in.

It can be extremely difficult to go against the majority—even if you know it is the right thing to do. There is a lot of pressure to be like everyone else. Have you ever gone against the majority to do what you believed was right? Why did you do it? Would you do it again? Why or why not?

What Might You Have Done?

Imagine you are working for President Dwight Eisenhower in 1957. Write a letter advising him what to do in response to the call for action in Little Rock. Respond to the President's belief that "I do not believe you can change the hearts of men with laws and decisions."

Political Propaganda

There are many ways in which politicians, advertisers, writers, and speakers try to persuade their audiences to agree with them. Sometimes authors use **propaganda.** Propaganda is the spreading of ideas in order to shape people's opinions. It is used to further the cause of one group or to damage that of another group. Often it will do both. Propaganda can contain half-truths and vague or misleading information. The following are some forms of propaganda.

Name calling. Name calling is used to damage the image or reputation of a person or idea. For example, a political candidate might call another candidate ineffective or dishonest.

Association. Someone trying to hurt an opponent's image might associate, or link, the opponent with an unpopular idea or cause. The association may not be truthful. It may also not be plainly stated. Instead, it might be implied, or hinted at. For example, if a relative of a politician has committed a crime, a political opponent may repeatedly draw attention to this crime in an attempt to discredit the politician.

Bandwagon. Bandwagoning is when someone tries to convince someone else to do or believe something because "everyone else is doing it." Bandwagoning is similar to peer pressure.

Glowing catch phrases. This idea represents something that many people favor, for example, a political candidate claiming to support the "American way." However, the candidate is not specific about what he or she means.

Critical readers pay careful attention to the words and phrases people use. Critical readers evaluate statements and arguments to determine if propaganda is being used.

On page 36 is the statement on integration made by Orval Faubus in his campaign for governor of Arkansas. Read the statement and the information that follows. Then think about how the author uses propaganda to make the reader agree with a certain point of view.

Recognizing Propaganda

Critical thinkers look for clues to help them recognize when propaganda is being used. Critical thinkers ask themselves questions such as the following:

- Who is giving the information? What is the purpose of the information?
- What are the facts? How are the facts proven?
- What audience is targeted by this information?
- What images and phrases are used? What is implied by the images and phrases?

Arkansas is not ready for a complete mixing of the races. Any attempt to solve this problem by pressure will hurt the good relations which exist between whites and Negroes. I am making my position clear to discourage those who might seek to play upon racial prejudice for selfish ends or, as in the case of communism, to create ill will between whites and Negroes.

Faubus used these arguments to oppose civil rights.

- Our community is not ready for "complete mixing of the races."
- We already have good relations between the races here in our community.
- People who favor integration are doing it for selfish reasons.
- Integration is a communist idea.

Now answer the questions below.

1. What is Faubus's point of view on integration?
2. Are there ideas that the author hints at but does not express openly? If so, what are they?
3. How can you tell that Faubus is using propaganda?
4. Write a speech opposing Faubus's ideas. Read your speech to a partner and have your partner read his or her speech to you. Give each other feedback that will help you make your points more clearly.

Copy the chart below on a separate sheet of paper. Then fill in the chart with examples from Faubus's statement. If he does not use a particular form of propaganda, simply write none in the box.

Forms of Propaganda Examples

Name calling	
Association	
Bandwagon	
Glowing catch phrases	

After a day's work, Rosa Parks wanted only to relax on the bus ride home. Her refusal to give up her seat to a white rider set off a movement that would inspire people all over the nation.

ROSA PARKS AND THE MONTGOMERY BUS BOYCOTT

CRITICAL QUESTIONS

- How did one woman set off the spark that ignited the Montgomery, Alabama, bus boycott?
- Why did ordinary people in Montgomery risk their jobs and their safety to boycott the city's buses?

TERMS TO KNOW

- theology
- nonviolence

ACTIVE LEARNING

After you have read this case study, you will be asked to work with a group of classmates to write a brief one-scene skit about the Montgomery bus boycott. At three points in this case study, Active Learning boxes suggest episodes that might make good scenes. These notes contain questions to keep in mind as you are writing your skit.

On the evening of December 1, 1955, a tired Rosa Parks boarded a bus in Montgomery, Alabama. The 42-year-old African American seamstress took a seat and began to relax. She had worked a full day on her feet. She had pinned up hems, ironed shirts, and carried dresses back and forth. Now at the end of the day, she looked forward to a relaxing ride home.

By law, the front seats of Montgomery's buses were reserved for whites. African Americans were required to sit in the back. In between was a small area where African Americans could sit as long as whites did not need the space. Without a second thought, Parks sat down in this area.

After a few stops, the white section of the bus was filled. The bus driver ordered Parks to give up her seat, but she said no, she was tired from working all day. The bus driver stopped the bus and ordered Parks and three other people to stand. The other people moved. Parks remained seated. "I'm going to have you arrested," the bus driver warned. Parks told the driver that he could do what he wanted. She wasn't moving.

The police arrived and arrested Parks. The police charged Parks with violating Montgomery's segregation laws. The soft-spoken Parks did not intend to violate the law that day. But by the time she left the bus, she had started a movement that would shake the nation.

Rosa Parks later spoke about her refusal to give up her seat. She said "The only tired I was, was tired of giving in."

Active Learning: One possible scene for your skit could show Rosa Parks on the bus. As she is being arrested, she might ask the police why they support the unjust Jim Crow laws. What kind of answer do you think the police would give her?

1 Running Out of Patience

Rosa Parks knew all about segregation. She had suffered from it all her life. As a child, Parks attended school for six months out of the year. For the other six months, she helped her grandparents, planting and picking cotton, peanuts, and other crops. Every morning, she saw shiny, new buses take the white students off to their shiny, new schools.

She was six years old when she first learned about the Ku Klux Klan. She heard her parents talking about the people that the Klan had beaten or shot. They were discussing homes and churches that the Klan had burned to the ground.

As an adult in Montgomery, Parks was highly respected in the African American community. She was an active church member and the secretary of the local chapter of the National Association for the Advancement of Colored People (NAACP). She also volunteered to work with youth groups and on community education projects.

Underneath her quiet manner, Parks had a deep, inner strength. Having felt the sting of injustice, she believed that she had a responsibility to help end an unjust system.

News of Parks's arrest quickly spread through Montgomery's African American community. Most African Americans had experienced unfair treatment on the buses. Many had been insulted by drivers. Often, after they had paid their fares, the driver would tell the African American passengers to get off the bus and board it by the back entrance. Sometimes, as they were walking to the back, the bus would pull away without them.

Planning the Boycott

Shortly after her arrest in the bus incident, E. D. Nixon, a leader in the local chapter of the NAACP, visited Parks. He told Parks that she

GOING TO THE SOURCE

Rosa Parks's First Brush with Segregated Buses

Twelve years before her arrest for protesting segregated busing, a bus driver threw Rosa Parks off a Montgomery bus for disobeying his demand to get off the bus and enter through the back door. Amazingly, the same driver who had her arrested in 1955 had thrown her off the bus in 1943. Here is her account of the 1943 incident.

Black people had special rules to follow. Some drivers made black passengers step in the front door and pay their fare, and then we had to get off and go around to the back door and get on. Often, before the black passengers got around to the back door, the bus would take off without them….[The bus drivers] carried guns and had what they called police power to rearrange the seating and enforce all the other rules of segregation on the buses. Some drivers were meaner than others. Not all of them were hateful, but segregation itself is vicious, and to my mind there was no way you could make segregation decent or nice or acceptable.

One day in the winter of 1943 the bus came along, and the back was crowded with black people. They were even standing on the steps leading up from the back door. But up front there were vacant seats right up to the very front seats. So I got on at the front and went through this little bunch of folks standing in the back, and I looked toward the front and saw the driver standing there and looking at me. He told me to get off the bus and go to the back door and get on. I told him I was already on the bus and didn't see the need of getting off and getting back on when people were standing in the stepwell, and how was I going to squeeze on anyway?

So he told me if I couldn't go through the back door that I would have to get off his bus…I stood where I was….

He looked like he was ready to hit me. I said, "I know one thing. You better not hit me." He didn't strike me. I got off, and I heard someone mumble from the back, "How come she didn't go around and get in the back?"….

I did not get back on the bus through the rear door….After that, I made a point of looking at who was driving the bus before I got on. I didn't want anymore run-ins with that mean one.

From *Rosa Parks: My Story,* by Rosa Parks.
NY: Dial Books, 1991 (pp. 77–79).

1. Give one example of the ways in which white bus drivers in Montgomery harassed African American passengers.
2. Why do you think Parks got on the bus at the front instead of the back?

had taken an important first step in the fight against segregation. But they would achieve nothing if she didn't fight the law.

Nixon knew that Parks had the strength to fight the case. But Parks's husband Raymond expressed the fear of many of Montgomery's African Americans. "Rosa, the white folks will kill you!" he said.

But Parks had made up her mind. She told Nixon, "If you think it will mean something to Montgomery and do some good, I'll be happy to go along with it."

Later that night, Nixon called Jo Ann Robinson, the president of an African American women's group. Robinson told Nixon that her group was planning a boycott of the buses.

Three quarters of Montgomery's bus passengers were African American. Nixon and Robinson knew that without these passengers, the bus companies would go bankrupt. Perhaps, they thought, this action would wake-up Montgomery to the injustice of segregation.

The two spent the rest of the night telephoning leaders of the African American community. Person after person agreed to meet that evening.

One of the first people Nixon called was the new minister of the Dexter Avenue Baptist

Thinking It Over

1. What plan of action did Jo Ann Robinson present to E.D. Nixon?
2. What warning did Raymond Parks give his wife?

Rosa Parks did not intend to violate the law. But she was willing to go to jail to stand up for her rights. Here, accompanied by her lawyer, Charles D. Langford, and a deputy, she is shown on her way to a Montgomery, Alabama, jail. She was jailed for "conspiracy to conduct an illegal boycott."

Church. He was a 26-year-old man named Martin Luther King, Jr. Nixon wanted to have the meeting at King's church. King agreed.

2 "Something Remarkable Was Unfolding"

Martin Luther King, Jr. was born in Atlanta, Georgia, in 1929. He grew up in a devout Baptist family. Both his grandfather and his father were ministers. King's grandfather led a protest to force Atlanta to build its first high school for African Americans. King's father spoke out for African American rights as pastor of the Ebenezer Baptist Church in Atlanta.

By age five, King could recite Bible passages from memory. By age 15, he had entered Morehouse College. By age 26, he had earned a Ph.D. in **theology**, the study of religion, from Boston University. In Boston, he met and married Coretta Scott.

When King was offered a post at the Dexter Avenue Baptist Church, he and his new wife felt torn. If they went back to the South, they would face the hated system of discrimination. Even worse, their children would come face-to-face with that system.

Yet the Kings still decided to return to the South. Both believed that they had a responsibility to help African Americans. Later King said that they "had the feeling that something remarkable was unfolding

Torn by conflict, Coretta Scott and Martin Luther King debated whether to return to the South. They knew they would face discrimination and expose their children, Martin Luther King, III, and Yolanda, to a cruel system of prejudice. In the end, both Kings decided that they had a responsibility to help Southern African Americans.

in the South, and we wanted to be on hand to witness it."

Active Learning: Another possible scene for your skit could show Martin and Coretta King deciding whether to take the position at the Dexter Street Baptist Church. What issues did the Kings have to face in making their decision?

King had studied the ideas of India's Mohandas K. Gandhi. Gandhi had waged a struggle to free India from British rule in the 1930s and 1940s. Gandhi had preached **nonviolence**, the peaceful refusal to obey unjust laws. King's study of history had convinced him that no one would win if African Americans used violence to protest segregation.

Throughout U.S. history, there had been frequent protests against injustice. But the protest that began in Montgomery, Alabama, in December 1955 was unlike many others. It was an example of nonviolent protest.

Thinking It Over

1. Why did Martin and Coretta Scott King hesitate to accept the post in Montgomery, Alabama?
2. What were Martin Luther King, Jr.'s ideas about the best course of social action?

Mohandas K. Gandhi was one of Martin Luther King, Jr.'s major inspirations. Gandhi led India's independence struggle by promoting nonviolence.

3 Striding Towards Freedom

The Friday night meeting that Nixon and King attended was brief. Everyone at the meeting was outraged by Parks's arrest. People wanted action of some kind. Nixon presented the idea of a one-day boycott for the following Monday. The group quickly approved the boycott.

But how would they inform Montgomery's African American community by Monday morning? It wouldn't help to hold a boycott that people didn't know about.

Volunteers printed leaflets urging people to join the boycott. "Don't ride the bus to work, to town, to school, or any place on Monday," declared one leaflet. Over the weekend, an army of volunteers handed out the leaflets all over town. Taxi companies owned by African Americans agreed to carry boycotters for the cost of the regular bus fare. Other people volunteered to form car pools.

The Buses are Empty

No one, not even Dr. King, was sure how effective the boycott would be. Montgomery's African Americans depended on buses to get to and from work. Would they be willing to take on all the hardships of giving up bus travel?

That morning, the Kings arose at about 5:30. A major bus route passed right by their house. The first bus was scheduled to pass by around 6 A.M. King was in the kitchen when his wife cried out, "Martin, Martin, come quickly!" She pointed out the window to a bus moving slowly up the street. It was empty. Twenty minutes later, a second bus passed. It was also empty. Fifteen minutes after that, a third bus came by. Only two white passengers

From Montgomery, the bus boycotts spread to cities throughout the South where segregation was a way of life. In Tallahassee, Florida, bus boycotters protested that city's segregated system. This car pool pick-up station allowed African Americans to get to work without using the bus system.

were on it. All that day, African Americans walked, rode in taxis or private cars, or thumbed rides. The boycott was almost 100 percent effective.

Most of Montgomery's African Americans did not own cars. But that Monday, they stayed off the Montgomery buses. The streets were crowded with African Americans walking to work. That evening, the streets were filled with people walking home.

Continue the Boycott?

The first day had been successful. But should the boycott continue? Wasn't it better to stop it on a high note than wait until the boycott fizzled?

King wasn't sure what to do. Like others, he worried that interest in the boycott would dwindle. He also worried about violence. Would African Americans give in to anger if whites cursed and beat them?

"There Lived a Great People"

That Monday night, King and Nixon addressed a meeting at an African American church. King and the other leaders had decided that the question of whether to continue the boycott would be determined at the meeting.

First Rosa Parks was introduced. The audience rose to its feet and cheered her for several minutes.

Several speakers then addressed the crowd. A group was formed to lead the boycott. It was called the Montgomery Improvement Association, or MIA. Reverend King later led the Association as president. Ralph Abernathy was another leader of the MIA. He was also pastor of the First Baptist Church in Montgomery. Abernathy became one of King's closest allies in the fight for equal rights.

King rose to speak to the crowd. He told the audience that he was glad it was Rosa Parks who had been arrested, "for no one can doubt the height of her character,

nobody can doubt the depth of her Christian commitment." Then he challenged the protesters. He told them that if they protested courageously, with dignity and Christian love that

> *when the history books are written in future generations the historians will say "There lived a great people—a black people—who gave new meaning and dignity to civilization."*

King told the marchers to keep walking. The boycott would go on.

A Good Movie to See

The Long Walk Home, New Vision Pictures. Van Nuys, CA: Live Home Video, distributed by Images Entertainment, 1991.

The Long Walk Home tells the story of the Montgomery bus boycott through the eyes of two women—a white woman and her African American maid.

The Walls of Segregation

The second day of protest proved just as successful as the first. Then another day was added; then another and still another.

At first, the boycotters demanded little. They asked only to be seated on a first-come, first-seated segregated basis. African Americans would be seated from the back. Whites would be seated from the front. No one would have to give up his or her seat to anyone else. They also requested that bus drivers be courteous to all passengers. Finally, they wanted African Americans to be hired as bus drivers on routes that served mainly African Americans.

Only the request for courtesy was accepted. "We have no intention of hiring niggras," the manager of a bus company said. A city official nodded in agreement. He said, "Come the first rainy day and the Negroes will be back in the buses."

Active Learning: A third possible scene for your skit could portray the moment when the boycotters presented their demands to Montgomery city officials and managers of the city bus companies. How do you think the officials and managers reacted to the demands?

The Walking City

The first rainy day came and the boycott went on. More rainy days came, and the boycott continued. Car pools were organized and churches purchased station wagons and drove workers to and from work. Leaders set up about 100 pickup stops across town to give workers rides to and from their jobs.

For more than a year, many of Montgomery's African Americans endured the hardships of walking nearly every place they went. One older African American woman turned down the offer of a ride saying, "I'm not walking for myself. I'm walking for my children and my grandchildren."

Some of the most determined boycotters were women who worked as cooks and cleaners for white families. Most of these women worked a great distance from where they lived. Each morning, these women woke before dawn so that they could walk to work. Many were threatened with the loss of their jobs if they did not give up the boycott. But the women refused to give in to threats.

The story of the bus boycott spread, help poured in. Donations, or money, came from all over the U.S. and as far away as Singapore and Japan. This support helped the boycott to continue through the winter. Montgomery became known around the world as "the walking city."

Bombs Thrown, Jobs Lost

Because the bus boycott was so successful, white authorities began to fight back. In January 1956, Rosa Parks lost her job at the department store. In February, police arrested Parks, King, and about 80 other boycotters. They charged them with "conspiracy to conduct an illegal boycott."

Police also arrested car-poolers for speeding—even when they were clearly under the speed limit. King, himself, was arrested for speeding and spent a few hours in jail.

As efforts to stop the boycotters increased, whites relied more heavily on acts of violence. They bombed four African American churches and two ministers' houses. A few days later, they threw a bomb into E. D. Nixon's front yard. Luckily, no one was hurt. Three weeks later, some whites threw a bomb at Dr. King's house. It exploded on his porch, shattering his front windows, and sending shards of glass throughout the house. An angry crowd of African Americans gathered in front of his house, but King calmed them.

> We must love our white brothers no matter what they do to us. If I am stopped, this movement will not stop, for what we are doing is right. What we are doing is just—and God is with us.

Thinking It Over

1. How did African American leaders spread word about the boycott?
2. Why were the leaders unsure about whether to continue the boycott?

4 "Glad to Have You With Us This Morning."

Spring came, and the boycott continued. A reporter interviewed one of the walkers. She was a tiny woman bent with age. "Aren't you tired?" he asked.

"My feet are tired," she said, "but my soul is rested."

By November 1956, the boycott had grown stronger. Sensing their new strength, the boycotters increased their demands. They were no longer willing to accept a place in the back of the bus. They wanted full equality.

They went to court to put the pressure on Montgomery. In May 1956, the boycotters filed a suit in federal court. The suit charged that Montgomery's system of segregated buses was illegal.

The Supreme Court heard the case brought by the boycotters that month. The Court unanimously outlawed Montgomery's bus segregation law. The Court found that segregation on buses was just as illegal as segregation in schools. But the city asked the Court to hear the case again, which delayed integration for a month.

The boycott lasted 381 days and nearly crippled the Montgomery bus companies. On December 21, King, Nixon, and other African Americans rode integrated Montgomery buses for the first time. The bus driver greeted them with a warm smile. "We are glad to have you with us this morning," he told them.

Leading the Movement

The success of the Montgomery bus boycott strengthened Dr. King's belief that nonviolent protest was the most effective tool for gaining civil rights. King quickly became one of the most important spokespersons of the Civil Rights Movement. In 1957, he joined with nearly 100 other church leaders in founding the Southern Christian Leadership Conference (SCLC). The SCLC's mission reflected King's ideas about protest: "To resist without bitterness; to be cursed and not reply; to be beaten and not hit back."

"It's Quite Interesting"

On the day that segregation on Montgomery's buses officially ended, some reporters interviewed Rosa Parks. They followed her as she took her first ride on a bus in more than a year. The last time she had been on a bus, she ended up in jail. This time, she sat back and enjoyed the ride. Always dignified, she refused to draw too much attention to herself. All she said was: "It's quite interesting to be on the bus again."

Others were not as reserved. All over town, African American men, women, and children rode in city buses. All enjoyed sitting wherever they pleased.

A white woman watched the scene that day. She had been on the side of the boycotters. She told a reporter:

The real power of the boycott was the Negro women. Every morning they came by our door here. It was like watching a brook to look out and see them going by steadily for an hour or so every morning, and an hour or so every evening.

Thinking It Over

1. What caused the Montgomery bus boycott to end?
2. What was the result of the Montgomery bus boycott?

Case Study Review

Identifying Main Ideas

1. What concern did leaders of the boycott have after the first day?
2. How did the demands of the boycotters change as the boycott got stronger?
3. What actions did people in the white community take when the boycott did not fizzle after the first few weeks?

Working Together

With a small group, find out whether there have been any boycotts in your community recently. If you cannot find a recent boycott in your community, study the role of boycotts in U.S. history. One well-known example of a boycott is the American colonists' boycott of British tea to protest the Stamp Act. Another example is the boycott of grapes in the 1960s and 1970s to support the strike of César Chávez's farm workers' union. Write a paragraph that summarizes either a boycott in your community or a boycott from U.S. history.

Active Learning

Creating a Skit Form a group with several classmates. Compare the notes you took while you read this case study. Choose a scene and write a brief narrative, or story, for it. Assign roles to the students in your group for each character in your skit. Practice the dialogue that you have written. Then, act out the scene for the class.

Lessons for Today

Review the "Working Together" activity above. Why do you think people participate in boycotts? What are the advantages of boycotts over other types of protest? What are the costs? Can innocent persons be hurt by boycotts? If you boycott an organization, should you prevent others from using that facility or product?

What Might You Have Done?

Imagine that you are asleep when a bomb explodes on your porch, sending glass shards throughout your house. Your friends appear with guns and clubs to find the bombers. Write an informal talk that you would give to your friends, guiding them in what they should do.

A White Person Fights the System

In 1955, a white minister named Robert Graetz became pastor of the Trinity Lutheran Church in Montgomery, Alabama. The members of Trinity Lutheran were mostly African Americans. The Graetz family chose to live in an African American neighborhood. When they went to movies, the Graetzes chose to sit upstairs in the African American section, rather than receive any of the benefits of segregation.

Graetz and his family found themselves rejected by the white community. The whites they met in the supermarket or the laundromat shunned them.

Graetz strongly supported the bus boycotters. In return, whites bombed the Graetz home—not once, but twice. Graetz was not frightened off, however. He continued to play a leading role in fighting segregation, both during the boycott and after.

Intellectual courage is the ability to keep an open mind and not allow others to make up your mind for you. You may have learned attitudes and beliefs that are false or misleading. It takes courage to question your own attitudes and beliefs.

By honestly considering other points of view, you remain fair. Being fair-minded helps you to recognize the truth, which is not always easy to do. Read the information in the sidenote on this page. Then respond to each question below.

1. Why do you think more white people did not attempt to help the striking Montgomery bus boycotters?

2. What qualities do you think a white Southerner would have as a person to help the bus boycotters?

3. If most of the people around you are sure of something, why is it difficult to question or disagree with them?

4. Why do you think it is difficult to question your own attitudes and beliefs?

Discussion

Throughout the South, Jim Crow laws took away the civil rights of African Americans. African Americans were prevented from voting by unfair rules. Today many people in the North and South can see how unjust this system was. Yet a half century ago, most whites in the South would have denied that the system was unjust. Why do people look at the system so differently today? Will people look back at conditions today and wonder why we once accepted them? Why or why not?

A white waitress stands behind a lunch counter with arms folded refusing to serve African Americans at an Oklahoma City diner in 1958.

SITTING IN FOR JUSTICE

CRITICAL QUESTIONS

■ Can store owners prevent people they don't like from shopping at their store?

■ What can people do to fight laws that they believe are unjust?

TERMS TO KNOW

■ sit-in

■ civil disobedience

■ picket

ACTIVE LEARNING

A storyboard is a plan of action. It consists of a series of cartoons or sketches. When movie directors plan a scene, they first draw it on paper. Then everyone has an idea of what the scene will look like *before* it is filmed. After you have read this case study, you will draw the storyboards for a film on the sit-in movement. The Active Learning boxes in this case study will give you ideas for several storyboard panels.

Imagine the following scene: You walk into a restaurant with a friend. Right away, you see that everyone is looking at you. People at the tables whisper to one another. You can see that some are even laughing at you. You sit down at a table. No waiter comes with a menu. You try to get service, but the waiters seem to be avoiding you. Then you see three men walking toward you. They are not waiters, and they don't look very happy.

"Uh-oh," you say to your friend. "This looks like big trouble."

In 1960, Ezell Blair, Jr., and three other teenagers experienced an incident similar to the one described above. Blair and his friends had angered some white people in Greensboro, North Carolina. In fact, the whites were so angry that Blair and his friends could have lost their lives. Instead, their actions set off a series of events that rocked the nation.

1 Breaking Down Barriers

The South had changed little since the *Brown* ruling of 1954. (See Case Study 1.) When African Americans broke the color barrier at Central High School in 1957, it seemed a great defeat for segregation. (See Case Study 2.) Yet by 1960, five Southern states had not even begun to desegregate their schools. More than 99 percent of African American students in the South still attended separate schools.

A Long Way to Go

Segregation in education was just part of the civil rights story. The Montgomery bus boycott of 1955–56 had stirred people across the country. (See Case Study 3.) Yet almost all public places across the South were still segregated.

In 1957, Congress had passed a law protecting a citizen's right to vote. Yet, in the South, few African Americans were registered to vote. African Americans who tried to register risked their jobs. Sometimes, they risked their lives.

A few protests did occur in 1958. For example, an African American teacher named Clara Luper led eight of her students on a lunch-counter **sit-in**, a type of protest, in Oklahoma City. Similar sit-ins spread to Wichita, Kansas. But that was as far as these protests went.

Segregation was strong throughout the South. African Americans could not eat at white-owned restaurants. They entered public buildings through side or back entrances. Whites used restrooms marked "Men" and "Women," while African Americans used restrooms labeled "Colored." Whites and African Americans were even buried in different cemeteries. White funeral notices were printed at the top of Southern newspapers; African American funeral notices were printed at the bottom. These conditions led Ezell Blair, Joseph McNeill, Franklin McCain, and David Richmond to act against segregation.

Deciding to Act

Blair and his three schoolmates did not rush into their decision to act. They often talked to each other in their dormitory at North Carolina's Agricultural and Technical College. They always came back to the realization that the Jim Crow laws were stronger than ever in Greensboro.

The four teens were impressed by the courage of the Little Rock Nine. (See Case Study 2.) They were awed by the people who had boycotted buses in Montgomery. Those role models led the teens to believe that direct action was the only way to break racial barriers.

For many nights, the teens talked about what they could do to oppose segregation.

Finally, they chose a plan. North Carolina, like all Southern states, had segregated lunch counters. One portion of each counter was reserved for whites; the other portion was for African Americans.

The four decided to sit at a whites-only lunch counter. They would start at F. W. Woolworth's store in Greensboro.

The four did not want to cause a disturbance. They thought that just sitting at the counter would show how senseless segregation was. "We'll stay until we are served," one of the students said.

Shaking Up Greensboro

On January 31, 1960, Ezell Blair asked his parents a strange question. Would they be upset if he stirred up trouble in town?

"Why?" his parents asked.

"Because tomorrow we're going to do something that will shake up this town," he replied.

At approximately 5:00 P.M. on February 1, 1960, Blair and his friends carried out their plan. They walked into F. W. Woolworth's. They bought a few items. Then they sat down at the whites-only lunch counter.

"Coffee, please," one of them said.

A waitress asked what they were doing at the whites-only counter. One of the students replied, "We believe we should be served."

The waitress called the store manager. He refused to serve the students. The four remained seated until the store closed. The next day, 20 students returned to sit at the counter. They stayed for a few hours. When the students left to attend classes, others took their places.

In 1960, segregation in public places was almost total in the South. The young people who sat in at the Woolworth's store in Greensboro, North Carolina, decided to take direct action to end racial barriers. Here, sitting at the "whites only" lunch counter in February 1960, four students protest segregation.

Two days later, 63 people crowded the same lunch counter. By Friday, more than 300 people were involved. Soon newspapers were calling the demonstration a sit-in.

As the news spread of the sit-in, reporters arrived to cover the story. A reporter asked one of the students why he was protesting.

"Segregation makes me feel unwanted," said 17-year-old Joseph McNeill. "I don't want my children exposed to it."

Thinking It Over

1. Why did the four Greensboro students decide to sit at the whites-only lunch counter?
2. What effect did previous civil rights protesters have on Blair and his friends?

2 Challenging the Heart of Segregation

Unlike earlier protests, there was no stopping this one. On the fourth day of the protest, white students from the University of North Carolina's Women's College in Greensboro joined the sit-in. Then similar sit-ins spread to other towns. A week later, a sit-in began in Durham, 55 miles away. Students from North Carolina College led this sit-in.

The Rising Tide of Protest

Then the protests spilled over into Tennessee. Students in Nashville and Knoxville started their own sit-ins. However, they did not just protest segregated lunch counters. These students also held sit-ins at movie houses, drugstores, libraries, and restaurants.

Soon, the sit-ins spread to the heart of segregation—the Deep South. This region included Georgia, Mississippi, Louisiana, Alabama, and northern Florida.

In late February, a sit-in began in Montgomery, Alabama. Before long, there were sit-ins all over the South. People in Florida, Georgia, Kentucky, South Carolina, Texas, and Virginia organized sit-ins. Thousands of students joined the rising tide of protest.

No central group directed the sit-ins. Yet the sit-ins had a common pattern. Most were led by college students. Some were even led by high-school students. Everywhere, the students were polite and peaceful. They simply asked for service. When whites would not serve them, they remained calm, but they didn't move.

Many of the whites who supported segregation were neither as polite nor as peaceful as the protesters. Instead they jeered at or dumped food on the students. They beat some of the protesters and even burned some with cigarettes. In the six months that followed the Greensboro sit-in, police arrested more than 1,600 young people.

Still, the protesters refused to strike back. When they were knocked down, they picked themselves up and got back on their seats.

Organizing Nonviolence

After a while, hundreds of sit-ins were underway. Student leaders met in Raleigh,

North Carolina, to form a committee to coordinate the activities. In April 1960, the students formed the Student Nonviolent Coordinating Committee (SNCC).

SNCC was based, in part, on Dr. Martin Luther King, Jr.'s ideas of nonviolence and **civil disobedience**. Civil disobedience is the act of breaking a law that a person thinks is unjust.

SNCC gave the protesters lessons in nonviolence. People who intended to participate in a sit-in learned how to protect their bodies if they were beaten.

Active Learning: You might use the "Sit-in Do's and Don'ts" to create a storyboard. Four panels of your storyboard could show the four "Do's" in the instructions for a sit-in. You might choose to create sketches showing a person practicing all the "Do's" suggested by the instructions.

Sit-in Do's and Don'ts

The students who took part in Nashville's sit-ins learned to be firm without being violent. They received the following instructions:

DO show yourself in a friendly way at all times.

DO sit straight and always face the counter.

DO refer all information to your leader in a polite manner.

DO remember the teachings of Jesus Christ, Mohandas Gandhi, and Martin Luther King, Jr.

DON'T strike back or curse back if attacked.

DON'T laugh out loud.

DON'T hold conversations with floorwalkers.

DON'T leave your seat until your leader has given you permission.

DON'T block entrances or aisles of stores.

Thinking It Over

1. What was the Student Nonviolent Coordinating Committee?
2. Do you think nonviolent measures were effective in the fight against segregation? Defend your answer.

3 "We Shall Overcome"

Under the leadership of SNCC, the protest movement took new forms. Students marched through town. They linked hands and sang spirituals. Of all the songs they sang, one spiritual stood out. Slaves had sung it a century before in their secret meetings. The spiritual expressed confidence that faith would lead them to victory.

A Good Video to Watch

Eyes on the Prize: America's Civil Rights Years, 1954–55. Boston, MA: WGBH.

This series of six videos examines the struggles for civil rights. Number 3, entitled "Ain't Scared of Your Jails," provides an exciting glimpse of the sit-in movement. The book, *Eyes on the Prize,* by Juan Williams, complements the video series.

Going to the Source

College Students Sit-In for Justice.

In 1961, a group of African American and white students sat down at a whites-only lunch counter in Jackson, Mississippi, and ordered food. A crowd soon gathered. A news photographer, called to the scene, took this picture. Study it and then answer the questions that follow.

The scene: a lunch counter in Jackson, Mississippi, in 1960. People around the world were dismayed by this picture. Peaceful demonstrators trying to be served at a Jackson, Mississippi, lunch counter, are doused with ketchup, sugar, and mustard by a cursing, leering group of young punks.

1. What does this picture show?
2. What do you think was the impact of this picture when people outside the United States saw it? What impact does the picture have on you?

The sit-in movement soon spread to the North. Here, demonstrators carrying placards gather in front of a Woolworth's store in Harlem in New York City. The demonstrators urged Harlem residents not to buy at Woolworth's until the store ended segregation at its lunch counters.

We shall overcome.

We shall overcome some day.

Oh, deep in heart, I do believe

We shall overcome some day.

"We Shall Overcome" became the anthem of the Civil Rights Movement. It became well known throughout the world.

Soon the sit-in movement spread to the North. Students in Northern cities **picketed** stores to support the civil rights protesters in the South. To *picket* means "to walk or assemble outside a place to publicize your cause."

Soon other types of sit-ins began, including "read-ins" in segregated libraries and "wade-ins" in segregated pools and beaches. There were even "kneel-ins" in segregated churches.

Active Learning: You could use the descriptions of the sit-ins to create three more panels in your storyboard. The panels could show the different types of sit-ins that took place in Southern and Northern cities.

To Break the Law or Not?

The tactic that the sit-ins used was known as civil disobedience. Not all African American leaders were pleased by the protesters' use of civil disobedience. Some, such as Thurgood

Marshall, were uncertain about the effectiveness of civil disobedience. Marshall had spent his life fighting against segregation in court. Many times he had also put his own personal safety on the line. No one could accuse Marshall of not supporting the Civil Rights Movement.

However, the sit-ins troubled Marshall. What would happen if large numbers of people involved in these sit-ins became violent? Shouldn't people fight these issues in courtrooms instead of in the streets?

Yet Marshall knew that the sit-ins were pushing progress. He saw that sit-ins raised legal questions. He could challenge these questions in court. In March 1960, Marshall called together 60 leading civil rights lawyers. As a result of the meeting, the National Association for the Advancement of Colored People (NAACP) took a firm position. It decided to help defend those who peacefully took part in sit-ins. Marshall said:

> If a dime store is open to the public, anyone who enters should get the same service as anyone else gets. The right of protest is part of our tradition. It goes back to tea dumped in Boston Harbor.

In the months ahead, the NAACP provided valuable legal help to sit-in protesters who had been arrested.

A Badge of Honor

Martin Luther King, Jr., and other leaders of the Southern Christian Leadership Conference (SCLC) gave students their support. In April 1960, King told a sit-in group that nonviolent protest was not only a way of integrating lunch counters, it was also a way to change the hearts of the people who supported segregation.

King said that the arrests for taking part in sit-ins were "a badge of honor." Over the next year, 70,000 students took part in sit-ins. About 3,600 received their "badge of honor" by serving time in jail.

After demonstrations in Nashville, Tennessee, SNCC leader John Lewis was pushed into a police patrol wagon and sent to jail. He was joined by 300 other protesters.

Thinking It Over

1. What does the term civil disobedience mean?
2. Do you think that civil disobedience is an effective way to change the law? Why or why not?

4 "The Sit-Ins Made It Ready"

Slowly, white merchants began to cave in under the power of the sit-ins. Lunch counters in Nashville and Greensboro began serving

African Americans. Other public facilities, such as restaurants, hotels, and other places, slowly became integrated.

By the end of 1961, stores in 114 cities agreed that they would serve all customers. "I used to say this town was not ready to desegregate," a white businessman said in Nashville. "The sit-ins made it ready."

New Leaders

The success of the sit-in movement created new, young leaders. One of the most determined was a Nashville, Tennessee, student named John Lewis. Lewis was one of ten children born to Alabama sharecroppers.

The sit-in movement brought new dynamic leaders to the fore. In March 1960, young Julian Bond led sit-ins at 10 restaurants in Atlanta, Georgia. A sit-in at Atlanta's City Hall made the nation aware of a new leader.

His family was very religious. Lewis began preaching at age four.

In the days of the Montgomery bus boycott, Lewis sat by his radio and listened to the sermons of Martin Luther King, Jr. King's religious faith gave Lewis the courage to risk arrests, jailings, and beatings.

Another young leader was Julian Bond. Bond was a 20-year-old student in Atlanta, Georgia. He helped organize a plan to support the Greensboro students. In March 1960, 200 Atlanta students held sit-ins in ten restaurants and lunch counters. Bond led a group into the whites-only cafeteria in Atlanta's City Hall. As they walked up the stairs, the group noticed a sign that read: "Public Is Welcome."

When they entered the cafeteria, the manager stopped them. "We can't serve you here," she said.

"That's not true," one of the students said. "You've got a sign outside saying the public is welcome. We're the public and we want to eat."

The manager called the police. The police arrested the student protesters, then released them later that evening. The protesters were eager to resume their work.

Bad for Business

The Civil Rights Movement became more powerful in the early 1960s. Many merchants feared that protests were "bad for business." They also worried about their cities' images in the media.

In the end, these fears proved to be important in ending segregation. For example, by the spring of 1960, merchants in some cities had integrated their stores to improve their image.

By the summer of 1960, 30 Southern cities had set up groups to review complaints of discrimination. On July 25, Woolworth announced that its Greensboro store would serve African Americans at the lunch counter.

But progress was slow. The sit-ins trailed off during the summer. They began again when school started in the fall of 1960. Sit-ins continued throughout the South for more than two years.

By the middle of 1961, restaurant and lunch-counter segregation was almost gone. Now, the young leaders looked for other ways to challenge segregation. Their next target was segregation on long-distance buses that ran between states. (See Case Study 5.)

By the end of 1963, about 930 protests had taken place. More than 100 Southern cities had been involved. More than 20,000 people had been arrested.

Civil rights protests also focused on other goals. One of the most important was registering people to vote. Another was getting the federal government to pass laws that would protect the rights of African American citizens.

The sit-ins had set off a firestorm of protest. Four college students had lit a spark by wanting to eat at a Woolworth's lunch counter. When other students pitched in, the fire blazed brighter. Then the fire spread across the state and to nearby states. Finally, it spread to the Deep South. When it finally ended, the South was a very different place.

The sit-ins hit white merchants where it hurt the most—in their wallets. As a result, many merchants gave in and soon integrated their businesses. They learned that integration was not harmful to business. In fact, it brought in customers who had never before shopped at the store.

More importantly, the student protesters showed that it was possible to bring about change through nonviolent means. They ended segregation by taking action and holding fast to their ideals.

Thinking It Over

1. Who were John Lewis and Julian Bond?
2. Explain what the businessman meant when he said, "I used to say this town was not ready for desegregation. The sit-ins made it ready."

Case Study Review

Identifying Main Ideas

1. The sit-in movement in the South began with the actions of Ezell Blair and his friends. Describe how the movement spread across the South and into the North.
2. How did the sit-in movement change after SNCC was formed?
3. (a) Why did Thurgood Marshall have mixed feelings about the sit-ins?
   (b) What stand did the NAACP eventually take on the sit-ins?

Working Together

Form a group with three or four classmates. Together, you will write and perform a brief skit about the sit-ins. Review this case study and choose one event or scene that your group would like to write about. First, create an outline for the script. Then write a first draft. Practice your skit and revise the dialogue and characters as necessary. Practice the skit several more times. When you feel comfortable with the script and your performances, present your skit to the class.

 ## Active Learning

Creating a Storyboard Put together the storyboard scenes you created as you read this case study. Use them to create a final presentation for your documentary. Review your storyboard. Then write a brief narration that links all the scenes. Present your storyboards to the class, reading the narration aloud.

Lessons for Today

The sit-ins of the 1960s created a new type of protest. Many protesters used sit-ins to protest causes other than segregation. In recent years, there have been sit-ins on streets, school grounds, and in government facilities. They have stopped work and disrupted transportation. Do you think it is right to disrupt the lives of people who may not have any involvement in the issue? Would this disruption help a cause? Write a brief essay explaining your point of view on this matter.

What Might You Have Done?

Imagine that you are one of Ezell Blair's parents. He has just told you that he is going to do something to "shake up this town." What questions would you ask him about his plans? What advice would you offer him?

The Language of Thinking

Criteria are rules, or standards, used to make a judgment, or decision. For example, your criteria for a good friend might be someone who listens to you or someone who makes you laugh.

Values are ideas, or beliefs, that are considered important. For example, some people may value friendship; others may value talent. Different people may have different sets of values.

Throughout our lives, we evaluate others' behavior and our own. We judge whether a certain action is good, bad, right, or wrong. An action that we decide is good or right is a moral action. In judging whether an action is moral, we consider such factors as the following:

- What are the circumstances?
- What is the law?
- What is the right action to take?
- What is the wrong action to take?

Opinions may differ about a certain behavior. Some people may think that a certain behavior is moral or immoral. Others might think it is neither.

Copy the graphic organizer below onto a sheet of paper. Use it to describe behavior that you think is moral and behavior that you think is immoral. Compare your completed organizer with someone else's. How are they alike? How are they different? How are your criteria different?

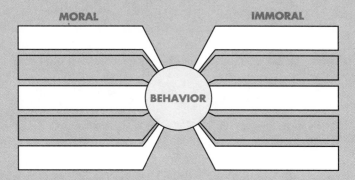

MORAL / IMMORAL / BEHAVIOR

Use your own ideas and the information you have learned about segregation to have a class discussion on the questions below:

1. Are the people who did not work to end segregation morally responsible for it? Give your reasons.
2. What might you do if you knew that something was wrong but were afraid to oppose it?

Under the soaring Washington Monument, Americans of all ages, skin colors, and religions met in August 1963 to demand equal rights.

FREEDOM RIDES AND FREEDOM MARCHES

CRITICAL QUESTIONS

■ Why were Freedom Riders willing to put their lives on the line to desegregate interstate buses?

■ How did some whites try to stop Freedom Riders and Freedom Marchers from protesting?

TERMS TO KNOW

■ interstate
■ reconciliation
■ Freedom Rides
■ suits

ACTIVE LEARNING

This case study focuses on the Freedom Rides and Freedom Marches. Three sections cover the Freedom Rides, the Freedom March in Birmingham, and the March on Washington. For each of these sections, you will be asked to conduct an imaginary interview with a person who took part in each event. Active Learning boxes appear several times to suggest subjects for the "interviews" and types of questions to ask.

Two young men—James Farmer and Bayard Rustin—got an idea. Farmer was the founder of the Congress of Racial Equality (CORE) in 1942. In 1947, five years after beginning CORE, Farmer and Rustin wanted to end segregation once and for all. They decided that they would begin by integrating **interstate** buses. Interstate buses ride across state lines.

Farmer and Rustin began to organize integrated bus rides throughout the South. However, it was still too dangerous in the 1940s to attempt integration in the Deep South. So Farmer and Rustin organized what they called "a journey of **reconciliation**." *Reconciliation* means "to make friendly again."

Farmer and Rustin's group rode public buses through Virginia, Tennessee, and Kentucky. At a number of stops, angry whites beat the riders. They even had Rustin arrested.

The beatings and jailings would have been enough to discourage most people, but not James Farmer. By 1961, Farmer had become a respected civil rights leader in Chicago. He decided the time was right for another attack on bus segregation in the South. This time, however, Farmer wanted to test segregation all over the South, including the Deep South. He even wanted to go into Mississippi and Alabama, where armed groups stood prepared to defend segregation. Farmer called his project the **Freedom Rides**.

1 Bound for Mississippi and Alabama

In May 1961, the first Freedom Ride began. A group of 13 African American and white volunteers boarded buses in Washington, D.C. Six riders rode in a Greyhound bus. Seven got on a bus run by the Trailways Company.

By custom, the front seats in the bus were reserved for whites. The back seats were reserved for African Americans. The African American Freedom Riders sat in the section reserved for whites. The white Freedom Riders sat in the African American section.

The Freedom Riders were bound for the two most segregated states in the nation—Alabama and Mississippi. Violent resistance to integration was the most widespread in these two states. The riders were testing whether the white South was ready to obey the federal law barring segregation on interstate buses.

All the Freedom Riders knew that what they were doing was extremely dangerous. Riders expected to be attacked. But they also considered the benefits should their plan succeed. They hoped to bring to the nation's attention the idea that, despite the law, whites still enforced segregation throughout the South.

A Calm Beginning

At first, the Riders had few problems. They rode through Virginia and North Carolina without any major incidents. The first problem arose when the bus reached Rock Hill, South Carolina. John Lewis, the young Student Nonviolent Coordinating Committee (SNCC) leader from Nashville, was the first person off the bus. "I knew it was going to be bad," he said. Trying not to show fear, he entered the "white" waiting room. Several white youths blocked his path. When he tried to walk past them, they clubbed him to the ground. Then a mob of whites savagely beat Lewis and two white Freedom Riders.

In Alabama, attacks on the Freedom Riders were even worse. At each stop, angry mobs of whites gathered. On May 14, Mother's Day, one bus stopped in Anniston, Alabama. White youths carrying sticks and clubs surrounded the bus. They slit two of the bus's tires.

The bus limped out of Anniston, followed by 40 cars filled with white "toughs." When the slashed tires went flat, the bus rolled to a stop. The riders waited inside the bus as the mob approached.

The angry crowd stormed the bus. They broke windows with rocks and clubs. They screamed curses at the Freedom Riders.

Eli Cowling, a white trooper from the Alabama highway patrol, was on the bus. Cowling moved to the door with his pistol in his hand. He held back the mob for more than 15 minutes. Then one of the mob threw a firebomb through a broken window. Genevieve Hughes was one of the Freedom Riders that day. She recalled:

> *A man thrust a bundle, seemingly of rags, through the window opposite me. At the same time he lit it. There was a noise. Sparks flew. A dense cloud of smoke immediately filled the bus. I thought it was only a smoke bomb and climbed over the back of the seat. The smoke became denser and denser. It became completely black.*

With handkerchiefs over their faces, the riders scrambled off the bus. As they got off the bus, the mob beat them.

Suddenly, a gunshot rang out. Eli Cowling warned the mob that he would shoot the next person who continued the violence. Convinced that Cowling meant what he said, the mob melted away.

Active Learning: Prepare at least five questions to ask someone who was on the Freedom Ride bus that the mob attacked in Anniston, Alabama.

The burned-out shell of a bus symbolizes the fury of mob hatred. On Mother's Day 1961, a group of white and African American Freedom Riders were attacked, beaten, and fire-bombed outside Anniston, Alabama. If the mob thought that this violence would end the integration campaign they were wrong.

Brutality in Birmingham

Meanwhile, the second bus rolled into Birmingham, Alabama. Another mob of whites armed with steel bars, bats, and chains waited at the Birmingham bus terminal for the bus to arrive. The U.S. Justice Department had asked the Birmingham police to protect the riders. But Police Chief Eugene "Bull" Connor did not care about orders from the Justice Department. He proved to be a narrow-minded bigot committed to defending the Jim Crow laws.

While the Birmingham police looked on, the mob beat the riders. When someone asked Connor why the police had not stopped the beatings, he said his officers had the day off in observance of Mother's Day.

But the riders came back. They boarded a bus bound for Montgomery, Alabama. Again the riders met with violence. Mobs cracked open heads and left Freedom Riders bleeding or unconscious. Once in Montgomery, the riders took refuge in an African American church. An angry mob outside the church threw rocks and burned cars. They broke the church's stained glass windows and tossed tear gas bombs into the church. Reluctant to get involved, the federal government waited until the last minute to send help. When federal marshals finally arrived, they drove off the mob and saved the 1,200 people inside the church.

All summer long, the Freedom Buses rolled into Mississippi. The police tried to stop the riders by sending them to jail. However, by the end of the summer, more than 300 Freedom Riders had come to the South. Half of them were white. By the fall, more than 1,000 people had made the dangerous journey.

All summer long, Freedom Riders rode through the Deep South. Their bravery forced the government to provide protection, such as these Guardsmen. In the end, Southern communities were forced to back down. By the end of the summer, even the Deep South had accepted integration on long-distance bus rides.

"Freedom, Freedom"

The violence against the Freedom Riders shocked the nation. It forced the Kennedy administration to act. Attorney General Robert Kennedy ordered federal marshals to protect the Freedom Riders. The riders headed into Mississippi, chanting, "Freedom!, Freedom!"

But the violence against Freedom Riders continued. Finally, the federal government issued tougher orders barring segregation in interstate travel. It also put more pressure on local communities to obey these rules. White Southern communities faced endless Freedom Rides—and federal government actions to enforce integration. As a result, most whites in Southern communities took down their "Colored" and "Whites" signs. Interstate travel was no longer segregated in the South.

But the Freedom Rides did more than just change laws. They gave the Civil Rights Movement a new spirit. They brought together people from the North and South—white and African Americans—to fight segregation. They inspired young people to join the movement. Most of all, they led the way for the next phase of the struggle—the Freedom Marches.

A Good Book to Read

Marching Towards Freedom, by Robert Weisbrot. NY: Chelsea House Publishers, 1994.

This book tells the story of the African American struggles for equal rights from 1957 to 1965. Chapter 3 on the Freedom Rides is particularly interesting.

came to Alabama to start a new round of civil rights protests. King planned to celebrate the 100th anniversary of the Emancipation Proclamation, the 1863 law that ended slavery, by marching through what King called "the most segregated city in America."

Breaking Barriers in Birmingham

Despite eight years of civil rights protests, Birmingham remained almost totally segregated in 1963. Whites continued to bar African Americans from using white water fountains, lunch counters, local buses, restaurants, and hotels.

Birmingham was large and enjoyed a booming steel industry. Yet few African Americans could find decent jobs. Most had to take low-paying jobs as servants or laborers.

The person upholding the Jim Crow laws was Police Chief Bull Connor. Connor warned that "blood would run in the streets of Birmingham" before he would agree to integrate the city.

To Martin Luther King, Jr., Birmingham was more than just a segregated city. It was the symbol of brutal discrimination against African Americans. King believed that a victory over segregation in Birmingham would

Thinking It Over

1. What happened to the Freedom Riders outside Anniston, Alabama?
2. How did Eugene "Bull" Connor try to stop the Freedom Riders?

2 Marching in Birmingham

On April 3, 1963, Martin Luther King, Jr., stepped off an airplane in Birmingham. He

Eugene "Bull" Connor led the white South's opposition to integration. Blaming the bloodshed on "out of town meddlers," he allowed his Birmingham police to stand aside while the Freedom Riders were brutally beaten. Why didn't his police protect the marchers? Because it was Mother's Day, he claimed.

inspire African Americans throughout the South to challenge the system.

King also knew that most whites in Birmingham would fight to preserve segregation. When city officials rejected demands for civil rights, King planned to stage a protest. He knew that Connor would viciously attack civil rights protesters. But King knew that the media—television, radio, and newspapers—would also be there. He anticipated that Connor's police would do something cruel in front of the television cameras. King would not be disappointed.

Freedom Now!

To block the protesters, Bull Connor had obtained a court order banning all demonstrations. King and the other leaders decided to go on with the march anyway. They knew that they were breaking the law. They also knew that the sole purpose of the ban was to support an unjust system. In defying the law, King was prepared to pay the penalty. He declared his willingness to go to jail to protest an unjust system. He told the marchers, "Make going to jail your badge of honor."

At first, the protests were peaceful. Relatively few African Americans were jailed. Then on Friday, April 12, 1963, King stepped onto the streets. Connor threw him in jail. For three days, Connor held King in solitary confinement in a small, dark cell. While he was in jail, a letter appeared in a Birmingham newspaper. The writers were eight white ministers from Alabama. They criticized the protests for "spreading hatred

Jailed for fighting segregation in Birmingham, Martin Luther King, Jr., wrote his eloquent "Letter from a Birmingham Jail" attacking injustice.

I am in Birmingham because injustice is here. Injustice anywhere is a threat to justice everywhere.

Then the letter attacked the idea that the protests had been hasty and had created bad relations between the races.

For years now I have heard the word 'Wait!'...This wait has almost always meant 'Never.'...When you have seen hate-filled policemen curse, kick and even kill your black brothers and sisters; when you see the vast majority of your twenty million Negro brothers in an airtight cage of poverty...; when you have to concoct [make up] an answer for a five-year-old son who is asking: 'Daddy, why do white people treat colored people so mean?'...then you will understand why we find it difficult to wait.

New Life

On April 20, King posted bail. But he did not leave Birmingham. Day after day, he and other civil rights workers marched. Even so, the campaign was not going well. Each day, the number of marchers got smaller. So many people had been arrested that the marchers were losing heart. After all their work, it was possible that the demonstrations might end in failure.

Then someone made a suggestion. Until then, the marchers had been adults. Why not allow high school students to march? Students would breathe new life into the movement. However, many of the older leaders did not want the young people to face the danger that awaited them.

In the end, the leaders decided to let students march. Although the young people would face danger, they faced far more danger if segregation continued.

On May 2, more than 1,000 young people joined the march. Young children joined their older brothers and sisters in marching through Birmingham streets for their rights.

Bull Connor did not care that the marchers were young people. More than 900 students

between the races." They called King an outsider.

King wasn't allowed to have any writing materials. But his lawyers smuggled a pen into the jail. Using the edges of newspapers and toilet paper, King wrote an open letter to the ministers. His "Letter from a Birmingham Jail" became one of the most important documents in the history of the Civil Rights Movement. King's supporters distributed more than a million copies of the letter to churches, newspapers, and political leaders.

"Letter from a Birmingham Jail"

In his letter, King first challenged the charge that he was an outsider. King said that injustice had nothing to do with being an insider or an outsider.

went to jail that day. The next day, about 1,000 more youths began to march. Police surrounded the marchers as they began to walk. Helmeted firefighters blocked the street.

"Turn on your water. Turn loose your dogs. We will stand here till we die," a minister cried out.

Bull Connor gave a signal. Immediately, the firefighters turned on the hoses. The high-pressure hoses swept marchers off their feet. The water knocked some people into buildings; it swept others into the street.

Then police dogs tore at the marchers' arms and legs. As protesters lay helpless on the ground, police beat them with clubs and dragged them into waiting wagons. Television cameras brought these horrible scenes to a national audience.

Two days later, thousands of marchers again took to the streets. When they reached the line of police and firefighters, the marchers knelt down to pray. Connor gave the signal to turn on the hoses, but nothing happened. The firefighters refused to turn on the hoses. They stood aside and let the marchers pass. The power of nonviolence had won the day.

Active Learning: If you could ask Bull Connor three questions, what would they be? Prepare three questions for an interview that you would hold with the Birmingham police commissioner.

A First Agreement

The protests began to wear down racist whites. Like the firefighters, many of Birmingham's business people were sick of the violence. They were even more alarmed at the way sales dropped in the city's stores. The African American community had launched an effective

Firehoses that knocked people over and stripped the skin off their backs was Bull Connor's answer to those who fought for racial justice in Birmingham. Hundreds of protesters were carted off to hospitals and jails.

boycott of segregated department stores. This seriously cut into sales and so did fear. Many people were afraid to shop downtown because of the violence.

In mid-May of 1963, protesters and city officials reached an agreement. The city agreed to desegregate lunch counters, restrooms, and drinking fountains. They also agreed to give African Americans more opportunities to get better jobs. In return, the protesters agreed to halt the demonstrations.

The agreement, however, did not end the violence. Bull Connor urged whites to reject the agreement. He tried to organize a white boycott of intergrated businesses. Bombs tore apart King's motel room and his brother's home. Connor's police force beat the crowds that gathered at the ruins.

But the agreement held. President Kennedy sent federal troops to patrol Birmingham. He also threatened to take over the Alabama National Guard to preserve law and order. An uneasy calm settled over the city. Birmingham accepted desegregation.

Thinking It Over

1. Why did Birmingham's civil rights leaders allow students to march in the protests?
2. What factors finally led to the success of the Birmingham protest?

---

3 The March on Washington

Events in Birmingham convinced President Kennedy to face the issue of civil rights. On June 10, 1963, the President addressed the nation. He demanded that Congress pass new civil rights laws.

The proposed bill, or law, called for an end to segregation in hotels, restaurants, theaters, and all other public places. It outlawed discrimination in any state program that used federal funds. It also gave the U.S. Justice Department the power to bring **suits**, or legal cases, against school districts that were not yet integrated.

A Tragic Murder

Kennedy's speech was cause for much celebration. But within 24 hours, tragedy struck. A young NAACP official from Mississippi named Medgar Evers was murdered. Evers was a leader in the struggle to gain civil rights for African Americans. He had spent the last few months organizing protests against segregation in Jackson, Mississippi. On the night of June 12, a sniper shot Evers outside his home.

The death caused outrage. In the end, it brought African Americans together to support Kennedy's civil rights bill. Civil rights leaders were determined to convince Congress to pass a strong set of laws. They decided to organize a mass march on Washington, D.C., to encourage public support for the bill.

The March

During August 1963, word of the march spread throughout the United States. From Harlem to Los Angeles, civil rights supporters packed their bags and headed to the nation's capital.

The people who arranged the March on Washington had hoped for a turnout of perhaps 10,000 people. On the morning of August 28, 1963, more than 250,000 people poured into Washington from around the country. They had come to pressure Congress into passing the civil rights bill. It was the largest demonstration for equal rights the country had ever seen. Around the world, millions of people watched on television.

GOING TO THE SOURCE

John F. Kennedy Calls for Equal Rights

On June 10, 1963, President John F. Kennedy spoke on nationwide television about the civil rights struggle. Kennedy was upset by the slow pace of change in Birmingham. He was disgusted by the violence. The following are several excerpts from his speech.

…This Nation was founded by men of many nations and backgrounds. It was founded on the principle that all men are created equal, and that the rights of every man are diminished [lessened] when the rights of one man are threatened….

The heart of the question is whether all Americans are to be afforded equal rights and equal opportunities, whether we are going to treat our fellow Americans as we want to be treated. If an American, because his skin is dark, cannot eat lunch in a restaurant open to the public, if he cannot send his children to the best public school available, if he cannot vote for the public officials who represent him, if in short, he cannot enjoy the full and free life which all of us want, then who among us would be content to have the color of his skin changed and stand in his place?…

One hundred years of delay have passed since President Lincoln freed the slaves, yet their heirs, their grandsons, are not fully free. They are not yet freed from the bonds of injustice. They are not yet freed from social and economic oppression. And this Nation, for all its hopes and all its boasts, will not be fully free until all its citizens are free.

From John F. Kennedy's *Public Papers of the Presidents of the United States.*

1. When President Kennedy said, "All men are created equal," he was quoting from the Declaration of Independence. Why do you think he quoted that document?
2. What is the "heart of the question," according to Kennedy?

In the Shadow of Lincoln

The crowd gathered on the mall of the nation's capital. It flowed around the Reflecting Pool and stretched from the Washington Monument to the Lincoln Memorial. Musicians played gospel music while the crowd assembled. Then civil rights leaders got up to speak. The last person to speak, and the person everyone had been waiting for, was Martin Luther King, Jr.

Standing beneath the giant statue of Abraham Lincoln, King delivered a brilliant speech. He spoke about unity and racial harmony. "I have a dream," said King, and the huge crowd erupted in cheers.

"I have a dream," he repeated. It was the dream that one day,

"I have a dream," Martin Luther King, Jr., said in words that inspired millions. His dream was an America where race simply didn't matter.

all of God's children…will be able to join hands and sing in the words of that old Negro spiritual: 'Free at last! Free at last! Thank God Almighty, we are free at last!'

A Civil Rights Act

The March on Washington showed Congress that there was widespread support for civil rights. Debate over the bill lasted for more than a year. During that time, President John F. Kennedy was assassinated. On November 22, 1963, a bullet took his life in Dallas, Texas.

It was left to the next President, a Southerner named Lyndon Baines Johnson, to win passage of the civil rights bill. In his first speech to the American people, Johnson said:

We have talked for 100 years or more. It is time to write the next chapter into the book of law. The need is now.

On July 2, 1964, Lyndon Johnson signed the new bill into law. Martin Luther King, Jr., and other civil rights leaders joined him for the ceremony. The fight for equality was far from over, but for the moment, the leaders enjoyed the victory.

Active Learning: Prepare a series of questions to ask someone who attended the March on Washington. The questions should explore what the March on Washington accomplished.

Thinking It Over

1. What event sparked the March on Washington?
2. How did the march affect passage of the civil rights bill?

Case Study Review

Identifying Main Ideas

1. What did the Freedom Riders accomplish?
2. Why did Martin Luther King, Jr., choose Birmingham, Alabama, as the focus of his 1963 campaign to end segregation?
3. What was the connection between the March on Washington and the Civil Rights Act of 1965?

Working Together

Form a small group. Create a mural about the Freedom Rides, the March on Birmingham, or the March on Washington. Decide which event to depict. Then create a list of possible scenes to represent the event. Sketch your ideas on a small sheet of paper and revise your images if necessary. Finally, transfer your mural to a large sheet of paper. Use original drawings or newspaper and magazine pictures for your mural.

Active Learning

Conducting Interviews Review the questions you wrote for each of the three "interviews" you would like to conduct. Work with another student in your class to write realistic answers to the questions. Then pick one of the three interviews and present it in class. Ask each question and allow your partner to answer. Based on your partner's answers, think of other questions you might ask the person that would help the class understand the Freedom Rides and Freedom Marches.

Lessons for Today

White opponents of integration argued that "strangers" had no right to tell Southerners how to run their communities. Is this argument fair? Did Martin Luther King, Jr., have a right to protest conditions in Birmingham? Does someone from outside your community have the right to protest against conditions in your community? Do you think someone from another country has a right to protest a situation in your community?

What Might You Have Done?

You are one of the leaders who has decided that students will be allowed to march in the Birmingham protests. Write a brief speech to the students describing the decision of the leaders and the reasons for the decision. Tell the students how they should behave and how they should protect themselves.

Examining and Supporting Your Opinions

Martin Luther King, Jr.'s, "Letter from a Birmingham Jail" energized the Civil Rights Movement. The letter stated the right of African Americans to equal treatment under the law.

Protecting the right to equal and fair treatment is an important responsibility of all citizens. One way in which you protect this right is through education. Once you have learned about your rights, you are better able to defend them. But when it becomes necessary, you can also protect your rights by going to court.

The term "civil rights" includes issues related to minority groups. Today's society is more sensitive not only to differences in ethnicity, but also to differences in religion, age, gender, and physical ability.

Most of us are in the minority at some point in our lives. At other times, we are part of the majority. For example, if you were the only male counselor at a summer camp for girls, then you would be in the minority. If you were one of only three English-speaking people in your classroom, then you would be in the minority.

When have you been in the minority? On a sheet of paper, list the times when you have been in the minority. How did you feel being in the minority?

Count the number of males and females in your classroom today. Record the number of each. Which group is in the majority? Which group is in the minority? In your opinion, are males and females treated equally at your school? Give examples to support your opinion.

Equality in School Sports

The U.S. Congress has passed many bills enforcing equal rights in the United States. For example, Title IX of the Education Amendments, passed in 1972, orders that all schools and colleges treat men and women equally.

Many schools have been criticized for not enforcing the Title IX law in their sports programs. In fact, many cases are coming to court that might force schools to provide equal athletic opportunities, facilities, and scholarships for men and women.

Read the sidenote, "A Case in Point." It is an example of women who fought for equal rights in college athletics.

Think about the sports programs in your school or in your community. Do they offer the same opportunities for both boys and girls?

Write a letter that expresses your opinion about this issue. The letter may either support or criticize a sports program or policy. You may write to a teacher, the principal, a physical education instructor or coach, or an athletic director. Before you begin, outline the reasons and examples that you will use in your letter. Then use the outline to write the actual letter.

Discussion

To meet the requirements of Title IX, many schools have had to eliminate certain boys' sports teams. Boys' sports teams, such as ice hockey, wrestling, lacrosse, and soccer, have been shut down so that the money can be used to fund girls' teams. Is this fair? What should a school do to be fair to all students in such a situation?

A Case in Point

Female athletes and their coaches at Colorado State University had tried for many years to get the university to create a women's softball team. The team the university had was for men only. Finally, the athletes filed a lawsuit claiming that the university's sports program was not treating men and women equally. As a result, a federal judge ordered the university to establish a women's team.

Supporting Ideas and Opinions

You know that it is important to use facts and details to support the main ideas in your writing. The quality of your writing depends on this practice. It is also important to use sound reasons and examples to support your opinions. The quality of your thinking also depends on this technique. Take time to think through your opinion and be prepared to give reasons and examples to support it.

In June 1964, three young civil rights workers disappeared in Mississippi. Their bodies were later found buried in a shallow grave.

FREEDOM SUMMER, 1964

CRITICAL QUESTIONS

■ Do you think the U.S. is a violent nation because of what happened in Mississippi?

■ What is the best way to win equal rights?

TERMS TO KNOW

■ volunteer

■ register to vote

■ literacy test

■ unseat

■ convention

■ delegate

■ compromise

ACTIVE LEARNING

You are the director of an advertising agency. One of your clients, a major television network, tells you that it is doing a week-long special about the events of Freedom Summer, 1964. The special will compare conditions in 1964 with conditions today. The network wants your agency to create a set of four posters. As you read, look for the Active Learning boxes to help you plan the posters.

On June 21, 1964, three civil rights workers left Meridian, Mississippi, in a car. They were headed for the town of Philadelphia, Mississippi. The three young men were on a fact-gathering mission. They wanted to explore reports that an African American church had been burned down because of its parishioners' involvement in civil rights activities.

Mickey Schwerner, a 24-year-old social worker; James Chaney, a 19-year-old student; and Andrew Goodman, a 20-year-old student, were the passengers in the car. Chaney, the only African American in the car, was from Mississippi. Goodman and Schwerner were New Yorkers who had come to Mississippi to fight against segregation.

Near Philadelphia, local police arrested the three men on a minor traffic charge and took them to jail. After several hours, a deputy sheriff released them. He warned the three to "get out of the state."

Missing

Other civil rights workers expected the three back in Meridian by 4 P.M. But late evening came, and they still had not returned. The civil rights workers became concerned. Finally, Bob Moses, the leader of the civil rights group, announced to his fellow workers that "three of our people are missing."

For six weeks, there was no sign of the three missing civil rights workers. Two days after they disappeared, FBI agents found their car. They discovered the car half buried in a swamp. The car had been badly burned. Six weeks later, FBI agents found three bodies buried under a dam wall. The three civil rights workers had been shot and brutally beaten.

After an FBI investigation, 18 white men were accused of the murders. An all-white jury freed 11 of them. Seven were found guilty on other charges. One of them was a deputy sheriff. The seven received sentences, ranging from three to ten years in prison.

People throughout the United States were shocked by the murders. But African Americans in Mississippi were especially angry. The three civil rights workers had given their lives in the fight to end segregation. Their murders showed just how brutal life was in segregated Mississippi.

Active Learning: The first of your four posters could refer to the murders of the three civil rights workers. Take notes on what your sketch will show. Plan what words you will use to make your point.

1 The Mississippi Summer Project

In Mississippi, fighting for equal rights was dangerous work. All civil rights workers knew that violence was common. Workers could face murders, bombings, fires, and mob attacks. Some whites wanted to send a clear message: "Do not tamper with segregation."

During the summer of 1964, civil rights workers decided to do more than tamper with segregation. They wanted to end it.

From all over the country, the Student Nonviolent Coordinating Committee (SNCC) attracted young people. Their message: "Come to Mississippi for the summer and help end segregation." The invitation soon led to the project that became known as Freedom Summer.

The Goals of Freedom Summer

The idea behind Freedom Summer was simple. About 1,000 **volunteers** would spread out over the state. A volunteer is a person who provides a service for free. Some volunteers helped to

Braving threats made by the Ku Klux Klan, young workers traveled from house to house registering African Americans to vote for the first time.

educate young people. Others helped adults **register to vote**. To *register* to vote means "to get your name on an official list of voters."

Most of the volunteers were white college students from the North. Others were African Americans from Mississippi.

The students who joined the summer project wanted to help the cause. One volunteer wrote on his application, "I want to work in Mississippi because I feel it is my duty

Active Learning: The second poster could show a message or slogan from civil rights workers. Make notes on what your message or slogan could be.

as an American to end segregation in this country." Another wrote, "I'm going because the worst thing after burning churches and murdering children is keeping silent."

Organizers of the project had several goals. They wanted to:

- start Freedom Schools for African Americans who were denied an education;
- help educate African Americans who lived in rural areas;
- work to increase voter registration; and
- build a new political party that would be open to all races.

Changing Mississippi

Mississippi was a natural place for an all-out attack on segregation. It was the poorest of all the states. It was also the state where many whites fought hardest against integration and civil rights. Between 1882 and 1952, Mississippi had 534 reported lynchings, more than any other state in the nation.

John Lewis, SNCC's chairman, said, "If we can crack Mississippi, we will likely be able to crack the system in the rest of the country."

Denied the Right to Vote

In the summer of 1964, less than ten percent of Mississippi's African Americans voted. This low voter turnout was the result of a racist system that used many tactics, or ways, to keep African Americans from voting. One tactic was to threaten violence. African Americans who tried to register to vote believed that they might get into trouble with the police. They were also harassed by racist groups, such as the Ku Klux Klan.

Another tactic racists used was economic pressure. Most African Americans worked for whites. Those who registered to vote could lose their jobs. A few African American farmers owned their own land. However, if they registered to vote, they would find it almost impossible to get the loans they needed to buy seed and equipment.

In addition, many African Americans were sharecroppers, living and working on land owned by whites. Most, therefore, lived in rented houses. Sharecroppers who registered to vote could be forced from their homes and thrown off the land. In Section 3, you will read how a white land owner ordered a woman named Fannie Lou Hamer off his land.

Thinking It Over

1. (a) Who were Mickey Schwerner, James Chaney, and Andrew Goodman? (b) What happened to them?
2. Why were most African Americans in Mississippi not registered to vote in the early 1960s?

---

2 Struggle in Mississippi

The Freedom Summer volunteers readied themselves for a tough battle during the summer of 1964. To prepare volunteers for their work, SNCC gave them a week of training. While the first group was in training, SNCC received the news that Schwerner, Chaney, and Goodman were missing. Feelings of fear and gloom swept through the volunteers. One volunteer remembered thinking:

> *What are my personal chances? There are 200 volunteers who have been working in the state for a week. Already three of them have been killed.*

But violence did not stop the workers. Every day, they eagerly went to work. They sang songs to keep up their spirits. When

A Good Video to Watch

Eyes on the Prize, Part 2: America at the Crossroads, 1965–85. Boston, MA: WGBH.

This second part of the well-known series is just as exciting as Part 1. Segment 2, "The Time Has Come," deals with Freedom Summer, 1964. It provides a glimpse of the barriers the volunteers tried to overcome during that summer.

someone's spirits were down, others gave support. They were workers on a mission—equal rights for all.

Anger and Welcome

The Freedom Summer workers were not welcomed by everyone in Mississippi. Some communities passed laws that made some civil rights activities illegal. For example, it became illegal to pass out leaflets calling for boycotts. Offenders could be sent to prison.

Racist and terrorist groups were also active. The Ku Klux Klan held open rallies. During rallies, speakers made violent threats against civil rights workers.

While most whites in the state were unfriendly, many African Americans welcomed the volunteers. The volunteers came to depend on the kindness and friendship of African Americans. They lived in the homes of African Americans and attended African American churches.

Freedom Schools

For many volunteers, their most important work was setting up Freedom Schools in

"Freedom Schools" in Mississippi taught reading, math, and other subjects to African Americans who were denied the right to a decent education. For the first time, students learned of people such as Sojourner Truth and Frederick Douglas who had left their mark on our nation's history.

Mississippi. These schools taught reading, typing, and other subjects. Few African Americans in Mississippi could get a decent education. They needed the Freedom Schools to break out of the hold of poverty.

The Freedom Schools were popular from the start. The students were dedicated and attended school, even when faced with danger. For example, one day racists firebombed the McComb Freedom School. Yet the next morning, 75 students showed up for class.

About 3,000 students attended Freedom Schools during the summer of 1964. For the first time, children learned about African American heroes, such as Frederick Douglass and Sojourner Truth. They also learned that the Supreme Court had outlawed school segregation nine years before.

The students eagerly took in this new knowledge. They realized that knowledge would give them the power to end segregation. Students debated whether to use violent or nonviolent tactics to end the injustices. They planned actions to integrate libraries and restaurants and learned about themselves. One student wrote the following poem:

> *What is wrong with me?*
>
> *Everywhere I go*
>
> *No one seems to look at me.*
>
> *Sometimes I cry.*
>
> *I walk through the woods and sit on a stone.*
>
> *I look at the stars and I sometimes wish.*
>
> *Probably if my wish ever comes true,*
>
> *Everyone will look at me.*

GOING TO THE SOURCE

A Southern Newspaper Attacks Freedom Summer

Almost all Southern newspapers resented the students who came to the South to work in Freedom Summer. A favorite tactic was to label them Communists. The following is an editorial that appeared in a Mississippi newspaper during the summer of 1964.

A thousand college students from the North are reported to be invading Mississippi this summer in order to engage in a Negro voter registration drive. It is unbelievable that a thousand college students would do this on their own. Those who know the ways of propaganda, especially of a Communist nature, probably correctly suspect that idealism of some college youngsters has been taken advantage of by some very hard boiled left-wingers and Communists who know exactly what they want to do—stir up trouble in the South.

It is of interest to note how, within almost hours after the disappearance of the first three civil rights agitators in the South, there were parades in Washington, Boston, Chicago, and in many other places across the land. If preparations had not been carefully made a long time ago for such demonstrations, they could not have come about so speedily.

This newspaper a long time ago pointed out that it is a deliberate attempt by Communist forces in the United States to stir up racial strife in this nation. The ultimate aim is, we believe, a black revolution. The invasion of Mississippi this summer is, in our estimation, part of this plan.

Entirely aside from the arrogance...of these students who are going to Mississippi with no knowledge of the Negro problem or how to handle the situation, the really serious aspect of this invasion of Mississippi is the fact that this is part of an overall scheme to destroy the United States by way of a racial revolution.

From the *Clarion Ledger*, Jackson, Mississippi, July 30, 1964.

1. Who does the newspaper say is taking advantage of the Freedom Summer students from the North?
2. What evidence, if any, does the newspaper cite to support its charges?

When Fannie Lou Hamer's landlord heard that she had registered to vote, he threatened to throw her off his land. Hamer replied: "I didn't register for you. I registered for myself."

Thinking It Over

1. What were Freedom Schools?
2. Reread the poem written by the African American student. What do you think the student meant by the last two lines?

3 Fannie Lou Hamer

Two years before Freedom Summer, a woman named Fannie Lou Hamer became involved in the Civil Rights Movement. Hamer's life had been difficult from the start. She was the youngest of 20 children born to poor sharecroppers. All her life, she had been working hard for little pay.

In the summer of 1962, Hamer went to a SNCC meeting, where she learned a surprising bit of information. "Until then, I didn't know that a Negro could register and vote," she said later.

After the meeting, she went to the courthouse to register to vote. A white official gave her a **literacy test**. This test is supposed to measure a person's ability to read and write. Only those who passed the test could vote. A literacy test can be difficult or easy. Hamer's test was very difficult. The official gave her complicated portions of the state constitution. He asked her to tell him what they meant. Displeased with her answers, the official told her that she had failed the test. She would, therefore, not be allowed to register to vote.

Hamer tried once more to register in December. An official again told her that she had failed the test. Finally, she succeeded in registering in January 1963. She was one of a few African Americans to successfully register. One African American took the test ten times and was rejected each time.

News of Hamer's registration soon reached her boss, the owner of the plantation on which she worked. The owner warned her: "Fannie Lou, we are not ready for this in Mississippi."

"I didn't register for you. I registered for myself," replied Hamer.

The owner ordered Hamer off his plantation. He warned her not to be seen near it again. He also threatened Hamer's husband "Pap." He said that if Pap Hamer went with his wife, he would lose his job.

Fannie Lou Hamer left the plantation that night. Her husband left soon after. Most people would have been frightened by the experience of losing a home and a job. However, Hamer reported that she wasn't scared.

What was the point of being scared? The only thing they could do to me was kill me. It seemed like they'd been trying to do that a little bit at a time ever since I could remember.

Hamer echoed the feelings of many when she said, "I'm sick and tired of being sick and tired." Those now-famous words became a motto of the Civil Rights Movement. From that point on, Fannie Lou Hamer became a leader in the voter registration campaign.

Hamer worked day and night to convince African Americans to vote. During the day, she walked in the fields with people. At night, she visited them in their homes. Her message was always the same: To make conditions better, African Americans had to put pressure on elected officials. They could do this only if African Americans could use their right to vote.

Hamer and other civil rights workers put their lives on the line to support their beliefs. In 1963, police arrested Hamer and three other African American women while in Winona, Mississippi. They were arrested on a trumped-up charge, that is a charge that is phony, or made up. The real reason that they were arrested was because of the roles they played in the voter registration drives. The police had badly beaten the four women. When they finally released Hamer from jail, she was half conscious and had to be taken to a doctor.

Active Learning: Your third poster should feature Fannie Lou Hamer. In your notes, plan what event in her life you will show. Plan what words you will use to make a point that grabs people's attention.

Voter Registration Drives

Stories similar to Hamer's were typical of the abuse civil rights volunteers suffered. Yet all through the summer, the volunteers continued to register African Americans to vote. They had a great deal of work to do. In fact, there were five counties in Mississippi with large African American populations. Yet none had a single registered African American voter!

The literacy test was one reason few African Americans were registered to vote. As in the case of Fannie Lou Hamer, white officials gave easy tests to whites and difficult tests to African Americans. Few people could pass the difficult tests given to them.

Another reason for the low numbers of voters was the threats African Americans received right before voter registration drives. Local papers published the names of those who applied to vote. This list made it easy for whites who were racist to harass African Americans who had dared to register.

Despite all the threats and violence, African Americans continued to register. In one town, an African American, who had lost a leg in World War I, went to the courthouse to register. In another town, a widow with ten children risked her job to register.

By the end of the summer, 17,000 African Americans had filled out voter registration forms. However, fewer than one in ten was actually able to register. Nine hundred of those who registered came from Panola County. There, a court had ordered U.S. government officers to supervise voting procedures. It seemed that Mississippi would allow African Americans to vote only if forced to do so.

Thinking It Over

1. What happened to Fannie Lou Hamer when she tried to register to vote?
2. What tactics did local officials use to keep African Americans from registering to vote?

4 Still Not Tired Yet

The cost of violence on African Americans during that summer was great. By mid-summer, Schwerner, Chaney, and Goodman were still missing. Most people believed they were dead. By the end of Freedom Summer, whites had burned 37 churches and bombed 30 houses and buildings. There were also 80 beatings. More than a thousand people had been arrested.

The violence did not stop the summer project. They moved on to the next phase—the launching of the Mississippi Freedom Democratic Party, or MFDP. The MFDP had been organized in April. It challenged the whites-only Democratic party in Mississippi.

Inside the MFDP

Everyone, regardless of race, could join the MFDP. Its goal was to **unseat**, or replace, the existing state Democratic party members at the Democratic National **Convention**. A convention is a meeting of members of a group. The most important goal of the Democratic convention was to select the person who would run for President on the Democratic ticket in 1964. The Democratic convention was scheduled for the end of August in Atlantic City, New Jersey.

The MFDP tried to get its people named as **delegates** to the convention in advance. A delegate is a person acting as another's representative. Their requests were rejected. The MFDP was not even allowed to take part in the state Democratic party meetings.

Holding the banner of the Civil Rights Movement, members of the Freedom Democatic Party keep an all-night vigil outside the 1964 Democratic convention in Atlantic City, New Jersey. The woman in the middle is Rita Schwerner, widow of the slain civil rights worker Michael Schwerner.

After these rejections, the MFDP decided to use a new approach. They began a campaign to get Mississippi voters to join the MFDP. To achieve this goal, they went to every church, business, and club in African American communities to recruit new members.

The Mississippi Democratic party was worried about the MFDP. Members feared that the new party would be seated, or would participate, at the Democratic National Convention. They used the power of government to oppose the party. Many MFDP leaders were arrested on minor charges to keep them from going to the convention.

"We'll Make You Wish You Were Dead!"

Fannie Lou Hamer, who had joined the MFDP, was one of the leaders who made it to Atlantic City. On August 22, 1964, she told the leaders of the Democratic party about the time she was arrested in Winona in 1963.

> It wasn't too long before three white men came to my cell. One of these men was a state highway patrolman. He said, 'We are going to make you wish you were dead.'
>
> I was carried out of that cell into another cell where they had two prisoners. The state highway patrolman ordered the first prisoner to take a blackjack [a leather-covered weapon].
>
> They had me lay down on a bunk bed on my face. I was beaten by the first prisoner until he was exhausted. After that, the state highway patrolman ordered the second prisoner to take the blackjack.
>
> All of this because we want to register, to become first-class citizens.

"Is this America?" she asked. "Is this the land of the free and the home of the brave?"

Hamer's speech aired on national television. Her story angered millions of Americans. Public opinion solidly supported the MFDP. The national Democratic party, from that point on, had to take the MFDP seriously.

Agreement—But at What Cost?

Leaders of the national Democratic party suggested a **compromise**. A compromise is an agreement in which both sides give in a little. The MFDP would receive two seats and the remaining MFDP delegates would be treated as guests. All Mississippi Democratic party delegates would be required to take a loyalty oath. They would support the person the Democrats named to run for President. A committee would make sure that all future delegations were integrated.

The MFDP delegates discussed the compromise. Finally, the Freedom Party voted that they would not settle for less than full representation. "We didn't come all this way for just two seats when all of us are tired," Hamer declared.

Disappointed, the delegates returned to Mississippi. They were discouraged, but as one member of the MFDP explained, they agreed to "regroup and come to fight another day." That is exactly what they did.

Four years later, at the 1968 Democratic convention, the MFDP challenged the Mississippi Democratic party. This time, the MFDP won. Thus, from 1968 on, Democratic National conventions were no longer segregated.

Active Learning: Your final poster will examine the conflict within the MFDP over whether to accept the compromise. Take notes on what you will show. Also take notes on the words that you will use to show the conflict.

Feeling Betrayed

In the fall of 1964, the leaders of SNCC, including Hamer, met in New York City to rethink their tactics. Many also began to question whether they really wanted integration. The leaders began to talk of separating themselves from whites.

Thinking It Over

1. What compromise did the national Democratic party offer the MFDP delegates for the 1964 convention?
2. Why did the MFDP reject the compromise?

5 The Long Hot Summer

In the heat of 1964, African American anger erupted. Fury focused on living conditions in the inner cities of the North.

The North had no Jim Crow laws, yet racism and segregation were widespread. White home owners would not sell to African Americans. African Americans were shut out of the best jobs. They were paid less than whites for the same work. The unemployment rate for African Americans was twice that for whites. Poverty and racism trapped African Americans in ghettos, or slum sections of cities.

These harsh conditions led some African Americans to lose hope. This loss of hope led to frequent acts of violence. There were also many acts of abuse by the police. All that was needed was a spark to set the cities ablaze.

Burning Wasteland

The first major disturbance began in Harlem, a large ghetto in New York City, on July 18. An incident between police and African American teenagers caused a riot where a 15-year-old student died. Before the rioting ended, hundreds had been killed.

Disturbances soon followed in Brooklyn and Rochester, New York. They spread to Chicago, Illinois; Philadelphia, Pennsylvania; Los Angeles, California; and several New Jersey cities. Rioters smashed and burned their own neighborhoods. Whole city blocks went up in flames. Many people, most of them African Americans, died.

A man in Los Angeles expressed his rage:

For years, we've been trying to get the mayor to come out and talk to us, but he wouldn't come. For years, we've been trying to get the governor, but he wouldn't come. For years we tried to get all those white folks downtown to come and pay some attention to us. But after we burned, baby, the whole world came to look at us.

President Lyndon Johnson tried to stop future rioting. He announced a "War on Poverty." The President's plan featured new federal programs to aid the nation's poorest citizens. But his efforts seemed too little too late. More trouble lay ahead in 1965.

Thinking It Over

1. What are ghettos?
2. What was President Lyndon Johnson's response to the urban disturbances?

Case Study Review

Identifying Main Ideas

1. What was Freedom Summer, 1964? What were its goals?
2. What were some of the lessons that African American students learned in Freedom Schools?
3. How did Fannie Lou Hamer fight against segregation in Mississippi?

Working Together

Imagine that next week you are making a speech to a group of community service volunteers. You want to use the example of the Freedom Summer volunteers to show the good work volunteers can do. In a small group, write a speech that you will give to the community volunteers, explaining what they can do on their own. Include some of the accomplishments of the Freedom Summer volunteers.

Active Learning

Drawing a Poster Review the notes that you took as you read this case study. Create four sketches for posters that use pictures and words to convince people to watch the television special your agency is making. It is not necessary to be a great artist to create the poster sketches. It is more important that you have a good idea of the message that you wish to convey.

Lessons for Today

To Fannie Lou Hamer, the right to vote was the key to winning her civil rights. Through voting, African Americans could put pressure on elected officials to respect the rights of all. Today Americans of all cultural groups, ages, and incomes vote less frequently than they did in the 1960s. What do you suppose is the reason for this lack of interest in or commitment to voting? How does it affect the country? What would increase interest among Americans to vote for their leaders?

What Might You Have Done?

"What was the point of being scared?" Fannie Lou Hamer said of the time when she was threatened because of her voter registration activities. "The only thing they could do to me was kill me. It seemed like they'd been trying to do that a little bit at a time ever since I could remember." Imagine that you are a poor farmer on the same farm on which Hamer worked. Hamer has come to you requesting your help in voter registration. What would you say to her?

Critical readers pay attention to a writer's choice of information. They consider what this choice might reveal about the author's point of view. Read the interview below. It was published in a Ku Klux Klan newsletter. This interview with a Klan leader took place shortly after FBI agents found the bodies of the three civil rights workers. After you have read the interview, think about how the author focused on particular ideas and left out other important information. The interviewer has asked why so many FBI workers were involved in the case of the missing civil rights workers.

> **A:** *First, I must correct you on your terms. Schwerner, Chaney, and Goodman were not civil rights workers. They were Communist Revolutionaries. They were actively working to undermine and destroy Christian Civilization. The outlandish [FBI] activity surrounding their case merely points up the political overtones of the entire affair...*

> **Q:** *By "political overtones" do you mean that the case has a bearing on the forthcoming elections?*

> **A:** *It is doubtful that the case itself will be made an issue in the election. However, the incumbent in the White House [President Lyndon Johnson] is a communist sympathizer, as proved by his numerous acts of treason...*

> **Q:** *Isn't it unlikely that the communists would do that [kill the civil rights workers themselves] in this case? Schwerner was a valuable man.*

> **A:** *Not at all. The communists never hesitate to murder one of their own if it will benefit the party.*

> From *Eyewitness: The Negro in American History,* William L. Katz. Fearon Education, 1974, pp. 501–2.

Use the chart on the next page to help you organize your thoughts. Copy the chart on a separate sheet of paper. In the circle, summarize the author's perspective of the Civil Rights Movement. Then in the boxes around the circle, write specific facts, details, or reasons that the author uses to support his view.

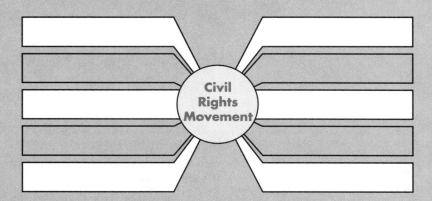

Sometimes people present a balanced perspective of people and events—that is, a fair, accurate, and complete description. Other times, they tilt the balance by including, or stressing, only certain information.

1. How does the Klan leader describe the civil rights leaders?

2. Would a civil rights worker describe Schwerner, Chaney, and Goodman the same way? Explain your answer.

3. Who does the Klan leader say murdered the civil rights workers?

4. Why would the Klan leader want to present the reasons for the murder of the civil rights workers in such a way?

5. Does the Klan leader's statement about the murdered civil rights workers fit with what you read in this case study? Explain your answer.

Discussion

The men brought to trial for the disappearance of the civil rights workers were not charged with murder. Instead the federal government charged the men with violating the rights of the civil rights workers. Why do you think the state of Mississippi did not bring murder charges against the men? What can citizens do to make sure that justice is served in similar murders?

Malcolm X sent a powerful message of solidarity and self-help that inspired African Americans throughout the nation.

THE BITTER STRUGGLE OF MALCOLM X

CRITICAL QUESTIONS

- How can a person who lives a troubled life get control of his or her life?
- Is separation or integration the right path for African Americans?

TERMS TO KNOW

- hustler
- recruit
- symbol
- mosque
- nationalism

ACTIVE LEARNING

Imagine that you are a brother or sister of Malcolm X. From your earliest days, you have kept a diary of your life and experiences. As you read this case study, you will receive a number of suggestions for writing diary entries about important events in Malcolm X's life. At the end of this chapter, you will use the entries to write a brief message on what Malcolm's life work meant to you.

On a cold, dark night in November 1929, two men silently crept up to a small frame house in Lansing, Michigan. The house was not much different from the other houses in the poor white section of town. It was a bit run-down, but neat. A small garden around the side of the house provided vegetables for the family. Bicycles and toys showed that children lived there.

The house might not have seemed all that special. But to the two men sneaking toward the house, it was very different. The people inside the home were African Americans. Almost everyone else in the neighborhood was white. The white men who approached the house did not want African Americans living in their neighborhood.

The Reverend Earl and Louise Little lived in the house with their five children. Reverend Little had become well known for his efforts to set up a strong African American rights organization. That alone made him very unpopular.

One of the children sleeping in the house that night was four-year old Malcolm Little. As an adult, Malcolm Little would write about this night in his autobiography. What he remembered most was the sheer terror he felt during the attack. The feeling would become deeply implanted in his memory.

> I remember being suddenly snatched awake into a frightening confusion of pistol shots and shouting and smoke and flames. My father had shouted and shot at the two white men who had set the fire and were running away. Our home was burning down around us. We were lunging and bumping and tumbling all over each other trying to escape. I remember we were outside in the night in our underwear, crying. . . . The white police and firemen came and stood around as the house burned down to the ground.

At the time, Malcolm Little was too young to understand why his house had been torched. He did not yet understand that he had been born into a world marked by racial hatred. But the understanding would soon come to him.

The child Malcolm Little would become the adult Malcolm X. He would spend much of his adult life trying to fight the racial hatred that had led people to burn down his house on that cold November evening in 1929.

1 Malcolm's Early Years

To understand the forces that shaped Malcolm X, we must first learn about a man named Marcus Garvey. During the 1910s, Garvey became well known in New York City's Harlem. Garvey had a vision of a new inner strength and independence for people of African descent from around the world. That vision won him the title, "Black Moses."

Marcus Garvey

Garvey started a movement that appealed to many African American people. He believed that equality with whites could come only through African American pride. Garvey argued that African Americans had to win economic, political, and cultural independence for themselves if they wanted equality.

In his native Jamaica in 1914, Garvey founded the Universal Negro Improvement Association (UNIA) to work towards independence for African Americans. "Up you mighty race!" he preached to African Americans. "You can accomplish what you will."

Garvey began a number of UNIA programs to help African Americans stand on their own. The UNIA newspaper, *Negro World*, carried stories about African American leaders and heroes usually left out of white newspapers. He argued that African Americans needed to rely on themselves, not on whites. African Americans needed to own their own businesses and land to gain equality in the world.

Later, Garvey expanded on his ideas. He argued that owning their own businesses and land was not enough. African Americans would still face prejudice in the United States. Therefore, Garvey called on African Americans to look to Africa as a model for inspiration. The accomplishments of Africans would stand as a spiritual beacon for people of African descent.

Programs like these won Garvey a huge following. By 1920, Garvey claimed to have more than four million followers. His critics, however, claimed that his numbers were overestimated. Still, Garvey was able to set up UNIA chapters all over the United States.

Trouble Over UNIA

Earl Little, a Baptist minister, was head of the UNIA chapter in Omaha, Nebraska. He was a tall, powerful man who was committed to improving the lives of African Americans. Little preached about winning civil rights for African Americans and opposing racial prejudice. He took an active role in helping the people in his parish.

Earl and his wife Louise had eight children. Malcolm, the fourth child, was born in 1925.

Reverend Little was a strong supporter of Marcus Garvey. He frequently led meetings in which Garvey's ideas were discussed. This alliance made Little popular among African Americans. However, it made him unpopular among whites. After threats by the Ku Klux Klan, the Little family was forced to leave Omaha and moved to Lansing, Michigan.

In Lansing, Reverend Little maintained his support for UNIA. Unfortunately, Little's troubles with whites also continued. In September 1929, the family was ordered out of their house because they were African American, but they refused to go. Two months later, as you have read, whites set fire to the Little family's house. Again, the Littles were forced to move to a new home, this time to one in an African American neighborhood.

In 1931, tragedy struck again. Reverend Little was found lying injured in the street. The police said he had been hit by a streetcar. The family believed that white racists had beaten him up. Little was taken to a hospital, where he soon died.

A Troubled Time

After Reverend Little died, the family faced difficult times. They had to go on welfare. There was never enough food for the family, and the Little children often went hungry. Malcolm remembered walking two miles into town with a nickel to buy a loaf of stale bread. Sometimes, things were worse.

> There were times when there wasn't even a nickel and we would be so hungry we were dizzy. My mother would boil a big pot of dandelion greens, and we would eat that.

Malcolm did well in school. He was a quick learner and eagerly grasped new material. He was also popular. He joined a variety of school clubs. Even though his school was mostly white, he was elected class president.

Then tragedy struck again, Malcolm's mother had a nervous breakdown. After his mother's illness, Malcolm was forced to live in a series of foster homes. Because of his family troubles, he went from being at the top of his class to dropping out of school.

Eventually, he moved to Boston, Massachusetts, to live with his sister, Ella. Malcolm started to get into serious trouble in Boston. He began drinking and taking drugs. Eventually, he got a job with a railroad company and traveled all over the east coast. When he reached Harlem, he was dazzled by what he saw and decided to move there.

In Harlem, Malcolm was drawn deeper into a life of crime. He sold drugs and started stealing. He became addicted to drugs and began gambling away all his money.

Later in his life, Malcolm took a hard look at what he had done in his youth. "I was a true

GOING TO THE SOURCE

Career Advice

Malcolm attended a junior high school in Lansing, Michigan, that was mostly white. He did well in school and was popular. One day, Malcolm had a conversation with one of his teachers. The conversation had a tremendous impact on Malcolm. In his autobiography, he called it "the first major turning point" in his life.

I know that he probably meant well in what he happened to advise me that day. I doubt that he meant any harm. It was just in his nature as an American white man. I was one of his top students, one of the school's top students—but all he could see for me was the kind of future "in your place" that almost all white people see for black people.

He told me "Malcolm, you ought to be thinking about a career. Have you been giving it thought?"

The truth is, I hadn't. I never have figured out why I told him, "Well, yes, sir. I've been thinking I'd like to be a lawyer." Lansing certainly had no Negro lawyers—or doctors either—in those days to hold up an image I might have aspired to. All I really knew for certain was that a lawyer didn't wash dishes, as I was doing.

Mr. Ostrowski looked surprised, I remember, and leaned back in his chair and clasped his hands behind his head. He kind of half-smiled and said, "Malcolm, one of life's first needs is for us to be realistic. Don't misunderstand me now. We all here like you, you know. But you've got to be realistic about being a Negro. A lawyer—that's no realistic goal for a Negro. You need to think about something you can be. You're good with your hands—making things. Everybody admires your carpentry shop work. Why don't you plan on carpentry? People like you as a person—you'd get all kinds of work.

From *The Autobiography of Malcolm X*
(New York: Grove Press, 1966)

1. What did Malcolm say he wanted to do with his career? What did Mr. Ostrowski advise Malcolm to do?
2. How do you think Malcolm reacted to this advice?

hustler," he later wrote. He said hustler is a small-time crook:

> *Uneducated, unskilled at anything honorable, I considered myself nervy and cunning enough to live by my wits. I exploited* [took advantage of] *any prey* [victim] *that presented itself. I would risk just about anything.*

A Dramatic Change in Prison

Malcolm later moved back to Boston where his life of crime continued. His cocaine addiction cost him $20 a day, a small fortune in those days.

He was arrested in January of 1946, and was sentenced to prison for burglary. While in jail, Malcolm changed dramatically. He met a fellow prisoner named Bimbi. Bimbi had educated himself and had the respect of the other prisoners.

Bimbi could see that Malcolm was intelligent. "Use your brain," he kept telling Malcolm. "Get an education."

Malcolm listened to Bimbi. He began to teach himself the rules of English grammar. He also read the dictionary to expand his vocabulary.

With his improved language skills, Malcolm began reading everything he could lay his hands on. He spent his days in the prison library.

Malcolm also improved his speaking skills by joining the prison's debating group. He was the best debater in the group. He carefully prepared his arguments and spoke forcefully.

Malcolm's brother Reginald visited Malcolm in jail. Reginald told his brother that he had joined a small religious group. The group was known as the Nation of Islam. Its leader was a man named Elijah Muhammad.

Malcolm listened carefully to his brother. He also continued his readings. Over a period of months, Malcolm became convinced of Elijah Muhammad's teachings. He began to write to Muhammad. In 1950, Malcolm joined the Nation of Islam.

The Nation of Islam

The Nation of Islam was popularly known as the Black Muslims. Elijah Muhammad had led the Black Muslims since the 1930s. He preached African American solidarity. He said that advancement in America could come only if African Americans helped themselves.

In 1946, Muhammad established his headquarters in Chicago, where he built up the group's membership. Members had to obey strict rules of personal behavior. They were not allowed to consume liquor or smoke tobacco. Muslims were also expected to dress neatly and to work hard.

Elijah Muhammad, the leader of the Nation of Islam, is shown on the group's newspaper, Muhammad Speaks. *Malcolm X saw in Muhammad's teachings a way to help African Americans gain control of their destinies.*

To Elijah Muhammad, whites were "blue-eyed devils." He instructed Muslims to avoid them. Muhammad's goal was to create a separate African American state. If this goal proved impossible, he felt that there should at least be strict separation of the races.

Thinking It Over

1. Who was Marcus Garvey? Why was his movement popular?
2. How was Malcolm's life changed by poverty and racism?

2 Taking Up the Challenge

In 1952, Malcolm Little left prison. He decided to go to Detroit. A number of his brothers and sisters lived there. He took a job in a furniture store where one of his brothers worked.

At night and on weekends Malcolm worked on **recruiting** new members for the Black Muslims. To recruit is to "get people to join a group or an organization." Malcolm made another important change. He discarded his last name, Little. According to the Black Muslims, Little was a "slave name" that whites gave to his ancestors. Malcolm replaced his last name with an "X." The "X" was a **symbol** of his missing African name. A symbol is a word, picture, or thing that stands for something else.

Working for the Nation of Islam

Within a few months, Malcolm X had tripled the number of members in the Detroit **mosque.** A mosque is a Muslim house of worship. He soon left his job at the furniture store to work full time for the Nation of Islam. His fiery speeches spoke directly to the despair felt by many African Americans, inspiring them to join the group.

In 1954, Elijah Muhammad sent Malcolm to Boston to recruit members. Three months later, he went to Philadelphia and organized a mosque there. He did so well that Muhammad made him head of the mosque in New York City. New York City became Malcolm's base. He attempted to look up people he had known during his criminal days. He found that most of them were either in prison or dead.

He also continued to travel throughout the country in search of new members for the Black Muslims. In less than ten years, Malcolm helped establish mosques in all 50 states.

Malcolm X became the most powerful speaker for the Black Muslims. He saw in Elijah Muhammad's teachings a way to help African Americans improve the quality of their lives in America. Malcolm X became well known throughout the country and the world. He appeared in newspapers and magazines, on radio and television. He was also invited to speak at famous universities.

A Message of Pride

During the 1950s and 1960s, the Nation of Islam movement grew swiftly in the urban ghettos of the North. There, many African Americans felt that the Civil Rights Movement did not have the answers to their problems. Although African Americans in the North could vote, travel on integrated buses, and eat in integrated restaurants, they still suffered from racial discrimination. Many were drawn to movements that preached black pride and black unity.

"Be proud of your black skin," Malcolm said. He insisted that African Americans could succeed only by helping themselves.

Malcolm was a fiery speaker. He spoke directly to the concerns of poor African Americans. He understood the tragedy of life

Operating out of a base from Chicago, the Nation of Islam built up a large following in the 1960s. Members had to obey strict rules of personal behavior. They were expected to dress neatly and work hard. The 1963 national convention, shown here, attracted African Americans from all over the United States.

in the Northern slums because he had lived there. He knew how African Americans resented their situation because he shared the same resentments. He knew of the terror of crime in the ghettos because he had been a criminal there. He knew that African Americans were angry at the way whites treated them because he shared that anger. To whites, Malcolm said,

> *What you don't realize is that black people today don't think it is any victory to live next to you or enter your society. This is what you have to learn—that the black man has finally reached the point where he doesn't see what you have to offer. Your own time has run out.*

Malcolm recruited thousands of new members for the Nation of Islam. Malcolm's message was to unite and win progress. African Americans should not want "to integrate into this corrupt society. They should separate from it, to a land of our own, where we can reform ourselves, lift up our moral standards, and try to be godly."

Thinking It Over

1. Why did Malcolm change his surname to "X"?
2. Why did many African Americans in the North think that the Civil Rights Movement did not offer solutions to all their problems?

Two uneasy allies meet in 1964. On the left Martin Luther King, Jr., greets Malcolm X in Washington, D.C., at a meeting on civil rights legislation.

3 A New Direction

While Malcolm X's popularity grew, Martin Luther King, Jr., continued the fight for civil rights. The two men chose different paths to help African Americans. The followers of Martin Luther King, Jr., sought unity among all Americans. The followers of Malcolm X sought unity among people of African descent throughout the world. The Nation of Islam looked to Africa for cultural traditions, including the practice of Islam.

The followers of Martin Luther King, Jr., wanted an integrated society. They believed that integration was the most important step toward gaining civil rights. The followers of Malcolm X believed that the only way to gain equal rights was to become economically independent.

Malcolm's followers preached black **nationalism**. Nationalism is devotion to a country or group. They revived the spirit of African nationalism inspired by earlier leaders like Marcus Garvey.

Dr. King's followers believed that nonviolence was the best way to win equality. Malcolm X pledged to win equality "by any means necessary." Malcolm did not preach violence. However, he said that violence was one way to win rights.

The Nation of Islam was not involved in any way in the Civil Rights Movement led by Dr. King. Malcolm X had no public praise for the sit-ins or the Freedom Riders. He refused to take part in the Birmingham marches. He bitterly criticized the March on Washington. He called it a "circus" and he said it had been taken over by whites.

Malcolm saved some of his most bitter words for leaders of civil rights activities. He attacked them for working with whites to achieve their goals. He said civil rights activists were more concerned with themselves than with African American people. He attacked Martin Luther King, Jr.'s "I have a dream" speech. Malcolm said that he saw no dream for African Americans. He only saw a nightmare.

The Split

Yet Malcolm changed over time. As he traveled across the world, he began to see new directions for the struggle. He began to question the Black Muslim belief that whites were "devils." He became convinced that the idea of a separate state was not realistic.

Malcolm was increasingly at odds with the Nation of Islam's leader, Elijah Muhammad. Malcolm had become the second most powerful person in the movement. As a result, other

Beginning with a hajj, or holy trip to Mecca, in 1964, Malcolm changed many of his ideas. He found many whites who showed no prejudice and treated him with kindness. Here he is shown meeting Egyptian leaders at Al Azhar University in Cairo, Egypt.

leaders became jealous of him. Malcolm was sure they were plotting against him.

In March 1964, he announced that he was leaving the Nation of Islam. He would form an organization of his own.

Trip to Mecca

Later in 1964, Malcolm made a hajj, or holy trip, to Mecca in Saudi Arabia. Mecca is the city where the Muslim religion began. It is the holiest city for Muslims.

Malcolm also traveled through Africa. He was deeply affected by the trip. He found whites who showed no prejudice. They entertained him in their homes and showed him acts of kindness.

Malcolm concluded that whites were not "devils." He found that they were not naturally evil. Rather, whites were influenced by the society in which they grew up. In Malcolm's view, the United States was a racist society. Therefore, whites grew up with racist ideas. Malcolm knew that he had called whites devils in the past. However, he said he would never again make such statements.

The change did not mean that Malcolm X was no longer frustrated. It did not mean that he was joining the civil rights struggle. He said:

> We are not fighting for integration. Nor are we fighting for segregation. We are fighting for recognition as human beings.

America's Only Hope

To destroy racism in America, Malcolm looked to the young people of the United States. "The

The part of Washington tourists saw was glitter and marble. But the part of Washington that most residents saw was rundown and very poor. As this 1967 photo shows, just 10 blocks from the U.S. Capitol people lived in crumbling frame houses. In the 1960s, the anger that slum residents felt exploded in a series of riots.

young whites, and blacks, too, are the only hope that America has."

Malcolm spoke to young African Americans. He urged them to think of themselves as part of an African majority, not an American minority. "There can be no black-white unity unless there is first black unity," explained Malcolm. "We cannot think of unity with others until after we have first united among ourselves."

Malcolm's travels had convinced him that African Americans and Africans were facing similar problems. Much of Africa was under the control of Europeans. Africans were struggling to break these bonds. They were fighting to establish their own nations. African Americans were also fighting to break the bonds of racism and trying to establish their independence.

Malcolm believed that black people on both continents should unite. If they came together as a group, they could better solve their similar problems.

Malcolm stressed self-determination by African Americans. "We won't get our problems solved depending on the white man," he declared. Only African Americans were allowed to join Malcolm's movement. He left the door open for cooperation with whites, however. Malcolm said that whites who wanted to solve the race problem should work with other whites.

Malcolm X attracted a large following. Many of these followers, however, focused on Malcolm's earlier message of anger towards whites. Most African Americans did not support Malcolm. Most favored the ways and beliefs of the civil rights leaders.

A Life in Danger

Malcolm X began 1965 with a new slogan: "Ballots or bullets." He focused on winning political power for African Americans, and he warned whites of a revolution if African Americans did not win such power. Malcolm X also let it be known that he would cooperate with other civil rights groups—and even whites—to achieve his goal. But he stuck fast to the need for a revolution in U.S. society.

Malcolm had made many enemies. He had turned his back on the separatism of the Nation of Islam. He believed that loyal followers of Elijah Muhammad might soon kill him for what they saw as his treason.

Malcolm became convinced that his life was in danger. For two years, he had been telling the story of his life to the writer Alex Haley. He pushed Haley to write the story down faster. Malcolm was convinced that he would not live to see his book published.

In late 1964, Malcolm learned that someone had given an order for his murder. On February 14, 1965, someone tossed a fire bomb through the front window of his home. It burned down half of his house. There was no insurance on the house. Now Malcolm had no home, no possessions, and little money.

On February 21, 1965, Malcolm X addressed a crowd of about 400 followers in the Audubon Ballroom in Harlem. Three men in the audience suddenly pulled out guns and opened fire. At 39, Malcolm X was dead.

Three men were arrested for the murder. Two of the three men were members of the Nation of Islam. They were tried and found guilty. All three served long terms in prison.

Malcolm was well known for only six years of his life. Yet, he is one of this century's most important figures. At his death, actor Ossie Davis said:

In honoring him, we honor the best in ourselves. . . . He was a black shining prince.

Thinking It Over

1. How did Malcolm's attitude toward whites change over time?
2. Why did Malcolm push the author Alex Haley to hurry-up work on his autobiography?

Case Study Review

Identifying Main Ideas

1. What steps did Malcolm Little take to change his life during his prison term?

2. (a) How did the ideas of Elijah Muhammad affect Malcolm X? (b) Why did Malcolm later leave Muhammad's Nation of Islam?

3. How did Malcolm X and Martin Luther King, Jr., differ in their approaches to fighting for the rights of African Americans?

Working Together

In small groups, choose an African American leader other than Malcolm X or Martin Luther King, Jr. Then research that leader's life. Write a two-page biography that includes that person's goals and achievements.

 Active Learning

Writing Diary Entries It is the day after Malcolm's murder. Reread the three diary entries you have written as you read this case study. Then put together a final, longer diary entry that uses the other three to sum up what Malcolm X's career meant to African Americans. Write a first draft of your final diary entry. After you read your first draft, revise it and prepare a final copy.

Lessons for Today

Malcolm's murder silenced his voice. But it did not silence his ideas. If anything, Malcolm's popularity has grown over the years. Violence against political leaders is an ever-present possibility. Why do people commit violence against political leaders? Why doesn't that violence have the effect the person who committed the violence wanted? Why does it sometimes make the murdered person's ideas even more popular?

What Might You Have Done?

It is 1944. You've come from Lansing, Michigan, to visit New York City on vacation. While in New York, you visit Harlem. Walking down the street, you meet Malcolm Little. Your older brothers and sisters know the Little family from the Lansing schools. Malcolm starts telling you about his life as a small-time crook. What might you say to him?

Comparing Ways to Protest

People often view the same event or situation differently. A person's point of view depends largely on his or her particular interests. For example, a heavy rainstorm would bother a person who wanted to go to the beach. It would ruin that person's plans for spending the day outside. However, a farmer might be very happy about the storm. It would water his or her crops and increase the farmer's chances of making money that year.

In the same way, people look at historical events from very different points of view. People who feel very strongly about an issue are often surprised to find out that a person on the opposite side of the issue can feel just as strongly. One of the most difficult tasks for a critical thinker is to try to "put yourself in the other person's shoes" and consider events from a different point of view.

The Civil Rights Movement, led by Martin Luther King, Jr., and the Nation of Islam had two very different ideas on how African Americans could gain equality. The followers of Martin Luther King, Jr., believed that equality would come about only if whites and African Americans worked together. The followers of the Nation of Islam, under the leadership of Elijah Muhammad, believed that advancement in the United States could come only if African Americans helped themselves. Elijah Muhammad's goal was to create a separate independent African American nation, or at least one where the races were separate. Look back in the case study to compare the two group's views on the best path to equality for African Americans.

Form groups of five with your classmates. Each member of the group should choose one of the following people to role play:

- Malcolm X before traveling to Mecca and Africa
- Malcolm X after traveling to Mecca and Africa
- A white person who supports the Civil Rights Movement
- Martin Luther King, Jr.
- An African American who lives in Harlem

Think carefully about the issue of the best path to equality for African Americans. To focus your thoughts on this issue, answer the following questions. Remember to answer the questions as the person you are role playing would answer them.

1. What would be the best way for African Americans to gain equality with whites?

2. Do you think that whites should help African Americans gain equality? If so, how should they do this? If not, why not?

3. What is your opinion of the Civil Rights Movement?

4. What is your opinion of the Nation of Islam?

As a group, have a discussion in which you present and compare your individual points of view on the best path to equality for African Americans. Remember that each of you is playing a role. Be sure that everyone has a chance to speak. After the discussion, answer the following questions.

5. In what ways were the views that were presented similar?

6. In what ways were they different?

7. Which point of view presented in this discussion comes closest to your own? Why?

Discussion

In trying to change attitudes toward the rights of African Americans, protest leaders argued that the way laws were made reflected racist views in society. Therefore, they argued, they did not feel bound to obey these laws. U.S. civil rights marchers went to jail rather than obey laws they considered unjust.

Think about how laws are made and what they mean. Is it ever right to break the law? If so, when is it right? When is it wrong? Should everybody who thinks that a law is unfair break that law? Should that person be punished for breaking the law? Explain your answer.

A more militant message and the black panther symbol of a new movement heralded a new era in race relations in the late 1960s.

BLACK POWER!

CRITICAL QUESTIONS

- How did the injustices that African Americans faced in the North differ from those in the South?
- In what ways did African American leaders disagree over the goals of the Civil Rights Movement in the 1960s?

TERMS TO KNOW

- militant
- grassroots
- exile

ACTIVE LEARNING

After you have read this case study, you will be asked to write a brief skit on the meaning of Black Power. The skit will have three scenes. There are Active Learning notes at three points in this case study. These notes suggest ideas that could be used to create the three scenes.

I wish there were a way to explain what it is like to be a Negro in the South. I wish I could explain what it is like to be a Negro moving down a deserted highway at night and see a car bearing strangers pulling out behind you. I wish I could put into words the sinking feeling in the stomach which can come over a Negro when he confronts a Southern sheriff.

The above quotation describes the fear African Americans faced in the segregated Southern states. The speaker was James Meredith. In 1962, Meredith became the first African American to enter the University of Mississippi. Angry whites rioted when Meredith first attempted to enter the university. The whites did not want African Americans in their school. In the end, federal troops were called in to escort Meredith safely to and from his classes.

After graduation, Meredith wanted to work against the fears he described above. He decided to bring public attention to the voter registration campaign in Mississippi. He wanted to encourage the state's nearly 450,000 African Americans to vote. Meredith planned to walk 220 miles from Memphis, Tennessee, to Jackson, Mississippi.

On a Sunday in June 1966, James Meredith and a handful of people set out on a public march. During the second day of his march, a white man stepped out of the bushes along the Mississippi highway. He had a shotgun in his arms.

"James Meredith," he said. "I want James Meredith."

When Meredith turned to face the gunman, the man raised his gun. Three shots rang out. Meredith dropped to the highway. He had been shot in the chest.

March Against Fear

The shots did not kill Meredith. He recovered after a long stay in a hospital. In the meantime, a number of civil rights activists came to Mississippi to finish the march he had started.

One of the civil rights activists was Martin Luther King, Jr. Another activist was a young man named Stokely Carmichael. Carmichael had just been elected head of the Student Nonviolent Coordinating Committee (SNCC).

The twenty-five-year-old Carmichael had a very different background from Dr. King. At 19, he had been a Freedom Rider. At 23, he ran a voter registration drive for SNCC in Lownes County, Alabama. At the start of the drive, not one African American was registered to vote in Lownes County. One year later, 3,900 had registered.

The voter registration marchers set out for Mississippi on June 7. King tried to rally crowds with the cry, "Freedom Now." Carmichael, however, used different words of protest.

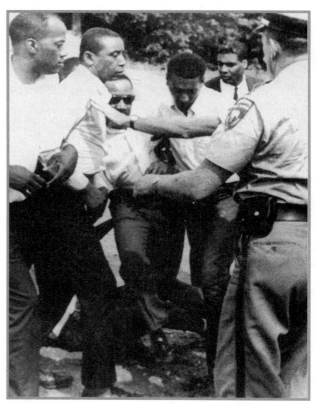

After James Meredith was shot, Floyd McKissick, Martin Luther King, Jr., and Stokely Carmichael led a march through Mississippi. Here, they have a confrontation with Mississippi state patrolmen.

Standing on a stage before a crowd in Greenwood, Mississippi, Carmichael said: "We've been saying freedom for six years, and we ain't got nothing." Then he coined, or made up, a new phrase: "What we're gonna start saying now is Black Power!"

At that moment, a SNCC worker jumped up on the stage next to Carmichael. He yelled out to the crowd, "What do you want?" The crowd yelled back, "Black Power!"

"What do you want?" he called out again.

The crowd exploded, "Black Power! Black Power! Black Power!"

For the rest of the march, instead of singing "We Shall Overcome," the crowd chanted, "Black Power! Black Power!"

1 Black Power!

"We Shall Overcome" had once been the anthem of the Civil Rights Movement. It represented a movement that fought for full equality with whites. The new chant "Black Power" became the slogan for people who had very different ideas and goals.

The concept of Black Power meant different ideas and goals for different people. For some, Black Power called for the establishment of African American political parties. Others believed it meant creating independent African American businesses. In the field of education, Black Power stood for local control of the schools in city ghettos. Wherever the ideology, or beliefs, of Black Power took hold, people began promoting programs of self-help and racial unity for African Americans. However, some people used it to authorize armed "self-defense" groups. Some even used it to justify looting and arson during urban disturbances.

Not all African American leaders supported the new slogan. Some urged Carmichael to stop using the phrase. Martin Luther King, Jr., thought the slogan sounded too much like a call for violence and separation.

Other African American leaders believed the slogan frightened whites away from the Civil Rights Movement. African Americans realized that they needed white support to get civil rights laws passed in Congress.

Roy Wilkins, the director of the NAACP, said, "Though it be made clear again and again, 'black power' can mean in the end only black death."

Active Learning: During the march from Selma to Montgomery, some of the marchers sang, "We Shall Overcome." Others chanted, "Black Power." Write a scene in which the marchers discuss the meaning of what they are chanting or singing.

Integrate or Separate?

But Carmichael refused to stop using the slogan. "Black Power!" became the chant of the new **militant** movement. *Militant* means "being aggressive and sometimes using force to fight for a cause."

In the past, Carmichael said that African Americans had tried to integrate into the mainstream. But integration had only helped a few individual African Americans. Instead of helping, integration had weakened the African American community as a whole. It kept African Americans dependent on whites.

Carmichael said that African Americans should not be fighting for integration. Rather, he declared:

The community must win its freedom while preserving its integrity [honesty]. This is the essential difference between integration and black power.

The struggle for equality was different in the North. No laws kept African Americans segregated. Yet, African Americans faced severe discrimination in the North. They faced poor housing, limited job opportunities, and high crime. Above, new "projects" under construction tower over slum housing in Chicago.

A Change in SNCC's Leadership

SNCC had led protests since the beginning of the sit-ins. The first leaders of SNCC had been activists, such as Fannie Lou Hamer and John Lewis. They were veterans of the civil rights struggle. They strongly believed in integration and nonviolence. Both looked to the leadership of Martin Luther King, Jr.

Other members, such as Stokely Carmichael, had very different beliefs. They believed in Black Power. Some, like the Black Muslims, argued for a separate nation. (See Case Study 7.) This nation would then work for its own goals, independent from white America.

By 1965, more SNCC members openly challenged Dr. King's leadership. Dissatisfied with King, some left SNCC to form an alliance with Malcolm X.

Several of the opposing groups' ideas were at odds with one another, for example, open conflict versus nonviolence and integration versus separation. No one knew which idea would be more successful or popular. The contest for leadership then moved to the North.

Thinking It Over

1. When was the slogan "Black Power!" first used in a public demonstration?
2. Why did Stokely Carmichael favor the separation of African Americans from white society over integration?

2 1965: A Year of Rage

African Americans in the North faced very different conditions from those in the South. Northern laws did not stop African Americans from voting or keep them out of restaurants, buses, and schools. They also did not directly prevent African Americans from getting good jobs or living anywhere they chose.

Yet African Americans still could not get good jobs. They continued to face discrimination in housing and education, which kept most African Americans in ghettoes. Although there were no Jim Crow laws, the spirit of Jim Crow was everywhere in the North. In Northern cities, poor families in ghettos struggled, not for civil rights, but for survival.

African American writer James Baldwin grew up in one of these ghettoes. He lived in Harlem, a large ghetto in New York City. As an adult, Baldwin recalled the condition of Harlem:

> *Everything was falling down and going to pieces. And no one cared. And it spelled out to me with brutal clarity* [clearness] *and in every possible way that I was a worthless human being.*

Ghetto life, Baldwin said, "caged me like an animal."

"Ghetto life," said the African American writer James Baldwin, "caged me like an animal." In the 1960s, some of the anger and frustration of ghetto life was released in a series of violent episodes in the nation's cities. Above, the National Guard patrols the Watts section of Los Angeles after six days of violence.

Watts Burns

On August 6, 1965, President Lyndon Johnson signed the Voting Rights Act. The act gave the federal government more power to fight discrimination in registration and election procedures. The act also outlawed literacy tests as requirements for voter registration.

Less than a week after President Johnson signed the act, an event took place that served as a reminder of the racism that African Americans faced every day. On August 11, 1965, California police in Watts, a Los Angeles ghetto, pulled over a man named Marquette Frye for drunken driving. When African Americans watching Frye's arrest saw one of the police pull a gun on Frye, tempers boiled over. By evening, thousands of rioters had filled the streets.

For six days, violence ripped through Watts. Cars and stores burned. Snipers shot at police and firefighters. Rioters destroyed nearly $45 million in property. As columns of smoke drifted up to the sky, angry African Americans shouted, "Burn, baby, burn!"

The nation had seen violence before. However, the disturbance in Watts still had a strong shock value. It showed, as no speech could, the rage ghetto residents felt about their treatment in U.S. society.

As Americans would soon see, the Watts riot was only the beginning. More violence in cities across America lay ahead. In the summer of 1966, there were riots in more than a dozen cities. National Guard troops were called into Chicago, Illinois; Cleveland and Dayton, Ohio; Milwaukee, Wisconsin; and San Francisco, California.

But the troubles that rocked 1967 made the 1966 riots seem small by comparison. In 1967, there were violent disturbances in Newark, New Jersey, and Detroit, Michigan. Some people considered the city of Detroit a model of good race relations. But that impression was just on the surface. Under the surface, African Americans were angry and frustrated with discrimination and racial inequality. "The Man's got his foot on my back and I can't breathe," said one unemployed African American in Detroit. A week after this statement was made, the city exploded in violence.

Civil Rights Falls Short

The Civil Rights Movement had not made a dent in the problems that African Americans faced in cities. The movement had integrated trains and restaurants in the South. But it had not been able to establish equal opportunity in housing, education, or employment.

Furthermore, the riots produced a "white backlash" against civil rights. Many white people turned against the movement. They claimed that African Americans were asking for too much or were asking for society to change too quickly.

Black rage over the white backlash fueled a new movement. It challenged the methods and ideas of whites and civil rights leaders. This movement was called "Black Power."

Active Learning: Write a scene that takes place about a week after the riots in Watts. A reporter comes into the neighborhood to investigate the disturbances. She wants to know the reasons why African Americans are so enraged. She interviews a neighborhood resident. For your scene, write three questions that she might ask and the answers that the Watts resident might give.

Thinking It Over

1. How was discrimination in the North different from discrimination in the South?
2. What message did Americans get from the riots in Watts?

GOING TO THE SOURCE

"It's Time Black People Got Together"

Stockely Carmichael was an African American leader who became frustrated by the slow pace of change in the mid-1960s. In the following 1966 speech, Carmichael outlines why African Americans had become impatient with the movement for equality.

I remember when I was in school they used to say, "If you work real hard, if you sweat, if you are ambitious, then you will be successful." I'm here to tell you that if that was true, black people would own this country. We have to say to this country that you have lied to us. We picked your cotton for $2.00 a day, we washed your dishes, we're the porters in your bank and in your building, we are the janitors and the elevator men. We worked hard and all we get is a little pay and a hard way to go from you.

Now there are a number of things we have to do. The only thing we own in this country is the color of our skins and we are ashamed of that because they made us ashamed. We have to stop being ashamed of being black. . . .

Now, let's get to what the white press has been calling riots. In the first place, don't get confused with the words they use like "anti-white," "hate," "militant," and all that nonsense like "radical" and "riots." What's happening is rebellion not riots. . . The extremists in this country are the white people who force us to live the way we live. We have to define our own ethic. We don't have to (and don't make any apologies about it) obey any law that we didn't have a part to make, especially if that law was made to keep us where we are. We have the right to break it.

From a speech by Stockely Carmichael on July 28, 1966.
In Notes & Comment (a newsletter by SNCC,
Chicago).

1. Why did Carmichael think that whites in the United States had lied to African Americans?
2. In Carmichael's view, who was responsible for urban disturbances in the 1960s?

3 Black is Beautiful

By 1966, SNCC was in turmoil. Young members wanted SNCC to set up programs in African American communities that were run by only African Americans. They also wanted to expel whites from the organization.

This removal of whites angered old-time members. Fannie Lou Hamer and John Lewis fought hard to allow whites to remain in SNCC. After an angry meeting, the Black Power members seized control of SNCC. John Lewis and Fannie Lou Hamer soon left the organization.

A new generation had seized control of SNCC. The differences between the old and the new groups were rooted in the lessons they had learned from their participation in the Civil Rights Movement. They had all worked at the **grassroots** level. *Grassroots* means "to work at the local level." They registered voters and taught at the Freedom Schools. While many civil rights activists still believed in racial integration, Black Power supporters no longer believed that whites would ever permit racial equality to occur.

The Words of Marcus Garvey

Almost half a century before the rise of the Black Power movement, Marcus Garvey had said:

> *If you cannot live alongside the white man in peace, if you cannot get the same chance and opportunity as a white man, then find a country of your own.*

Garvey was an important inspiration for the new movement. Stokely Carmichael, among others, studied Garvey's words. Carmichael and members of the new Black Power movement updated Garvey's message for the 1960s.

Carmichael argued that African Americans did not truly want to be merged into white

Active Learning: During a meeting of SNCC, an argument breaks out between two sides. One side supports Stokely Carmichael. The other side supports Fannie Lou Hamer and John Lewis. Write a scene in which several members of the opposing sides confront one another after the SNCC meeting.

society and that whites would not allow the races to integrate. He said that African Americans should stand apart from whites and be their own people.

Carmichael's ideas found an eager audience among many African Americans. Frustration, poverty, and prejudice drove many African Americans to embrace his words of racial pride.

Revisiting Their Roots

A new slogan took hold—"Black is Beautiful." Interest in studying the African American experience inspired the slogan. An important part of that experience was the community's roots in Africa.

Many African Americans wanted to know more about Africa. Some made journeys to Africa. Others influenced schools and colleges to create African studies courses. In these classes, students learned about African history, art, music, and literature. The courses helped African Americans to learn about their heritage and to find a new sense of pride. Even hairstyles changed as African Americans began wearing a natural "Afro" look.

African Americans also began learning about their culture in the Americas. "Black Studies" programs began in colleges across the country. These courses explored the diversity of African American life.

The Black Panthers

In Oakland, California, in 1966, two young African Americans started what was known as the Black Panther party. Huey Newton and Bobby Seale created the Black Panthers in order to tear down the barriers facing African Americans.

Their answer for breaking existing racial barriers was a militant political party. The Black Panthers demanded that African Americans control the centers of cities where primarily African Americans lived. They demanded that the federal government rebuild decaying city ghettoes. The Panthers said that this improvement would repay African Americans for the years of slavery that they were forced to endure.

Panthers demanded that African Americans be freed from jail and tried again by African American juries. The militant group also called for armed rebellion, if necessary, to win its goals.

Not everyone knew about the Panther's political ideas. But nearly everyone recognized what they wore: black trousers, black leather jackets, blue shirts, and black berets.

The Panthers received an enormous amount of publicity. Almost everyone knew of their activities. The Panthers accused the police of trying to wipe them out. Armed groups of Panthers clashed with police in city after city. Police shot and killed a number of Panthers during raids.

Membership in the Panthers was always low. By the end of the 1960s, the Panthers were crippled as a group. Most of the leaders were dead, in jail, or in **exile**. *Exile* means "being forced to live in another country."

"Two Americas"

After the summer disturbances in 1967, President Johnson appointed a commission to explore the roots of the trouble. Illinois Governor Otto Kerner headed the group, known as the Kerner Commission.

The commission's report was solemn. It said that white racism was responsible for inequality in housing, education, income, and a difference in life expectancy between whites and African Americans. The commission blamed the police for the deaths in the ghetto uprisings. It said that neglect, job discrimination, lack of decent housing, and poor educational opportunities caused the disorders. According to the Kerner report:

> *Our nation is moving towards two societies. One black, one white, separate and unequal.*

The Kerner Commission report described the United States as a society with deep social and economic differences between African Americans and whites. White racism caused these differences and fueled the anger of the Black Power movement.

In the words of African American politician Barbara Jordan:

> *The Civil Rights Movement called America to look at itself in a giant mirror. Do the black people who were born on this soil, do they really feel this is a land of opportunity, the land of the free. America had to say no.*

Dressed in black pants, leather jackets, and black berets, the Black Panthers became a familiar part of the Black Power movement. Their protest activities made front-page news. Not everyone, however, knew of their other activities, such as the teaching of African American history in Oakland, California.

Jordan's words echoed the thoughts and feelings of many African Americans and whites. The Civil Rights Movement had achieved a number of victories. But bringing true equality to Americans of all races was a goal that had yet to be reached.

Thinking It Over

1. What issue philosophically divided Fannie Lou Hamer and Stokely Carmichael?
2. How did the ideas of Marcus Garvey influence Black Power leaders?

Case Study Review

Identifying Main Ideas

1. How did the march that took place after a white man shot James Meredith reflect splits in the Civil Rights Movement?
2. What were the causes behind the disturbances in Watts in 1965 and the other urban disturbances of the 1960s?
3. How did the goals of the Black Power movement differ from those of Martin Luther King, Jr.?

Working Together

The movement to include Black and African studies in colleges encouraged many African Americans to examine their own family histories. In his book, *Roots*, author Alex Haley explored the African backgrounds of his ancestors. *Roots* inspired many people to trace their own family roots. With a group, discuss what you know about your family's history or the history of a friend's family. What events in U.S. history did members of the family witness or take part in? Do any family members remember the Black Power movement or the Black Panthers?

Active Learning

Creating a Skit Study the three scenes that you created from the Active Learning notes in this case study. Then write a brief introduction to each scene. Make sure that each scene relates to Black Power themes. Work with several of your classmates to perform some of the scenes for the class.

Lessons for Today

Discuss the methods African Americans used to improve their conditions. Think about something in your school or community that you would like to improve. Then create a plan of action. What have you learned from the Civil Rights and Black Power movements that could help you make the changes you want?

What Might You Have Done?

Imagine you are a member of the Board of Directors of the Student Nonviolent Coordinating Committee (SNCC) in 1966. A debate is going on between the "old timers," such as John Lewis and Fannie Lou Hamer, and the "young hawks," such as Stokely Carmichael. The two sides come to you for support. What might you say?

Differing Criteria

Critical thinkers base their evaluations on sets of standards called criteria. Critical thinkers try to develop criteria that are fair and balanced.

Each individual has his or her own criteria for evaluating events and ideas. This difference in criteria is one of the main reasons that people often disagree about important topics, such as politics. Although they may explain their points of view clearly, people do not always convince each other that their way is the correct one.

Compare and contrast... are words that often appear in the textbooks you use. Critical thinkers understand ideas that seem similar on the surface, but are actually quite different. On the other hand, opposing ideas may have a lot in common.

By 1966, Carmichael's Black Power group had taken control of the Student Nonviolent Coordination Committee (SNCC). Civil rights leaders, such as Fannie Lou Hamer and John Lewis, opposed most of the ideas put forth by Stokely's group.

Review the information about the two groups in this case study. Then answer the following questions.

1. Which group called for using violence, if necessary, to gain equality?

2. (a) How did Stokely Carmichael's Black Power group feel about integration? (b) How did they feel about working with whites?

When you have answered the questions, copy the Venn diagram below on a separate sheet of paper. In the part of the circle on either end, list the differences between Stokely Carmichael's Black Power group and the old leadership of SNCC. In the area where the circles overlap, list what the two groups have in common.

Discussion

With a group of your classmates, discuss the similarities and differences between members of the Black Power movement and SNCC members who supported the old leadership.

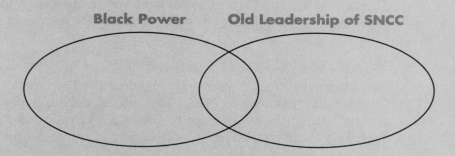

Black Power   Old Leadership of SNCC

The Civil Rights Movement encouraged millions of Americans to stand up for what they knew to be right and to take control of their fate.

THE ROAD PARTLY TRAVELED

CRITICAL QUESTIONS

- How did the death of Martin Luther King, Jr., affect the Civil Rights Movement?
- Has the prediction of the Kerner Commission come true? Has the U.S. become "two societies"?

TERMS TO KNOW

- assassin
- institution

ACTIVE LEARNING

This chapter clarifies the historical record of the Civil Rights Movement. It also links the civil rights era with the present. For your Active Learning project, you will write questions for interviews with present-day experts in fields related to the Civil Rights Movement. The subject of the interview is the meaning of civil rights today. Use the information in the Active Learning boxes to help you prepare for your interview.

By 1967, Martin Luther King, Jr., believed that the nation's main enemy was poverty. He said that poverty led to violence. In the 1960s, there was plenty of violence in the streets of U.S. cities. The United States was also involved overseas in the Vietnam War.

King attacked the country's role in the war. He referred to the conflict as "one of history's most cruel and senseless wars." According to King:

> The war is doing far more than destroying the hopes of the poor at home. We are sending black young men to guarantee liberties in Southeast Asia which they have not found in East Harlem. On TV, we have watched Negro and white soldiers die together for a nation that has been unable to put them together in the same schools. I speak for the poor of Vietnam whose country is being destroyed. I speak for the poor of America who are paying the double price of smashed hopes and death and corruption in Vietnam.

Active Learning: How do you think Dr. King's view of the Vietnam War affected the attitudes of people in the United States toward the war? Write five questions to ask an expert today.

At a funeral ceremony in Atlanta, Coretta Scott King and the King children stood by the coffin of Martin Luther King, Jr. His tombstone echoed his words at the March on Washington: "Free at last, free at last, thank God almighty I'm free at last!" Of course, African Americans were not yet free.

1 The End of an Era

To end the violence, the nation needed to wipe out poverty. As a way to combat the problem, King began building what he called the Poor People's Campaign.

The Poor People's Campaign

King planned to start his campaign to end poverty in April 1968, with a march on Washington. That spring, he traveled around the nation trying to increase support for his cause. Among the cities King visited was Memphis, Tennessee. His goal there was to support a strike by the city's garbage workers.

On April 3, King addressed a Memphis crowd. He told the crowd that he had received threats on his life. But he explained that he was not frightened because, he said, "I've been to the mountaintop and I've seen the glory." King was referring to the future; a future free of discrimination and racism. He then described his vision of a world free of poverty. "I may not get there with you," he continued. "But I want you to know that we as a people will get to the promised land."

The next afternoon, King stood on the balcony of his motel room. He was joking with members of his staff. Suddenly, a shot rang out. King fell. A bullet had torn through his jaw. An hour later, the leader who dared to dream of peace between the races died. He was 39 years old.

King's **assassin**, or murderer, was James Earl Ray. Ray was a white man. King's murder set off a burst of fury among African

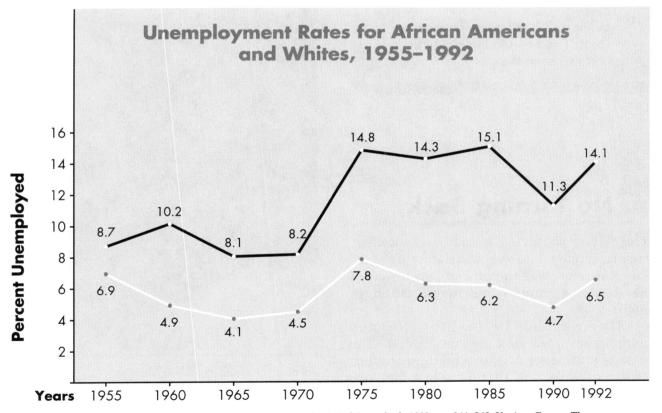

Unemployment Rates for African Americans and Whites, 1955–1992

African American: 8.7 (1955), 10.2 (1960), 8.1 (1965), 8.2 (1970), 14.8 (1975), 14.3 (1980), 15.1 (1985), 11.3 (1990), 14.1 (1992)

White: 6.9 (1955), 4.9 (1960), 4.1 (1965), 4.5 (1970), 7.8 (1975), 6.3 (1980), 6.2 (1985), 4.7 (1990), 6.5 (1992)

Sources: Garwood, Alfred N., ed., *Black Americans: A Statistical Sourcebook, 1992*, pp. 241–242; Kurian, George Thomas, *Datapedia of the United States, 1790–2000*, p. 76; Smith, Jessie Carney, et. al., eds., *Statistical Record of Black America*, 1995, p. 739.

Americans. Disturbances broke out in cities throughout the country. President Lyndon Johnson attempted to calm passions. By addressing the nation, he hoped to stop the riots. The President said, "I ask every American citizen to reject the blind violence that has struck down Dr. King, who lived by nonviolence."

King was buried in an African American cemetery in Atlanta, Georgia. His tombstone read:

> Free at last, free at last, thank God almighty I'm free at last.

The world that King left behind, however, was anything but free.

Thinking It Over

1. How did Martin Luther King, Jr., die?
2. What did Dr. King mean when he said: "I've been to the mountain top and I've seen the glory"?

2 No Turning Back

"Our nation is moving toward two societies, one black, one white—separate and unequal." This statement was the official conclusion of the Kerner Commission's investigation in 1968.

During the 1970s, the Kerner Commission's warning became clearer. The average income for African American families remained about half that for white families. In 1975, unemployment among African Americans was 14.8 percent. Unemployment among whites stood at 7.8 percent.

Some Gains

The differences between African Americans and whites remained a problem for African Americans. Yet they did not forget the advances that the Civil Rights Movement had made over the years. Because of the movement, Supreme Court decisions officially ended legal segregation. The movement was also successful at integrating schools and other public facilities. The Civil Rights Act of 1964 was the most sweeping civil rights legislation since the Reconstruction. It protected voting rights and banned segregation in public places. Furthermore, the act withheld government funds from programs that practiced segregation.

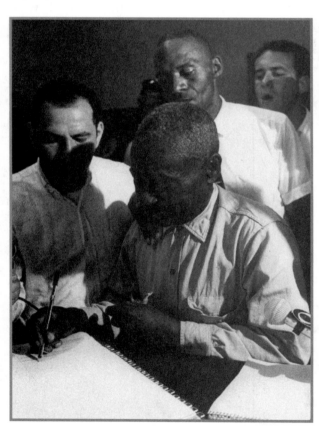

As a result of the Freedom Marches, Torn Flowers was able to register to vote in Batesville, Mississippi in 1966. Flowers, aged 68, voted for the first time in the election of 1966.

The Voting Rights Act of 1965 was just as important. It outlawed literacy tests as requirements to voter registration. The act gave the federal government the power to take over voting and registration procedures, if the local authorities discriminated against citizens. Effective voter registration drives gave African Americans the power to help shape their future by actively taking part in elections.

The most important effect of the movement was that it exposed flaws within U.S. society. White Americans could no longer pretend that the blessings of liberty were equally available to every citizen.

Because of the Civil Rights Movement, people learned how to work for change. The movement was so successful that other groups adopted its tactics. Women, the disabled, and other ethnic groups all began to protest for their rights.

As African Americans more fully participated in society and politics, the number of elected African American officials increased significantly. Between 1970 and 1975 alone, the number of African American politicians elected to office doubled. For the first time, African American mayors took office in large cities. Atlanta, Detroit, Los Angeles, and Newark all elected African American mayors.

Active Learning: If a member of the Kerner Commission were to visit your school, what five questions would you ask the commissioner about the predictions made in the report?

People all over the United States, inspired by the successes of the Civil Rights Movement, began to use the same methods to promote their own causes. Under the leadership of César Chávez, center, Latino farmworkers in California organized successful sit-ins and freedom marches.

Under Fire

By the late 1960's, the war in Vietnam had divided Americans at home. Many African Americans supported the Vietnam War. They viewed military service as a patriotic duty.

The heroism of African Americans in Vietnam was critical in the war effort. For example, army nurse Dorothy Johnson cared for the wounded while pinned down under mortar fire. Air Force pilot Major James T. Boddie, Jr., flew more than 153 missions over North and South Vietnam in only seven months. Milton Olive lost his life when he threw his body over a live grenade to save the men in his squad.

A Changed Military

The exemplary service of African Americans during the war brought major changes to the U.S. military. More African Americans enrolled in service academies. For example, in 1973, 46 African American cadets joined the first-year class at the Air Force Academy in Colorado Springs, Colorado. In 1963, the academy did not have any African American cadets.

African Americans also successfully broke into the top ranks of the military. In 1969, the army promoted 27 African American soldiers to colonel. By 1971, the army had 12 African American generals. In 1971, the navy made Samuel L. Gravely, Jr., the first African American admiral in U.S. history.

The extent of the advances African Americans had achieved became clear when the nation entered its next major war. In 1991, the United States and several members of the United Nations went to war against Iraq, a country in the Middle East. At that time, General Colin Powell, an African American, was Chairman of the Joint Chiefs of Staff. This position is the highest in the nation's armed forces.

General Powell successfully led U.S. forces in defeating Iraq. He is now a highly repected leader in the nation.

Active Learning: Write five questions to ask an expert about the changing role of African Americans in the military.

Thinking It Over

1. How has the role of African Americans in the military changed over the years?
2. Why did Martin Luther King, Jr., oppose the war in Vietnam?

3 A Dream Not Yet Fulfilled

The Civil Rights Movement of the 1950s and 1960s changed the United States forever. African Americans could no longer be forced to eat in separate restaurants or sleep in separate hotels. The days when African Americans were forced to ride in separate sections of buses and trains were also over.

More importantly, African Americans would no longer be prevented from voting. Until 1964, only about 40 percent of the South's African American adults were registered to vote. In Mississippi, that figure was about five percent.

With the right to vote came the power to elect public officials. By the early 1990's, two thirds of all African Americans in the South were registered to vote. There were more than 7,000 African American elected officials. Mississippi, alone, had more than 600 African American officials. In addition, there were 24 African American members of Congress.

African Americans had served as the mayors of 30 U.S. cities. The three largest, New York, Los Angeles, and Chicago, had all had African American mayors. Across the country, African Americans held elected offices in state and local governments.

In the world of work, progress was slower for African Americans. But some barriers had fallen. In business after business, African Americans held jobs that once only white people would have held. To get higher paying jobs, increasing numbers of African Americans were graduating from colleges and professional schools.

I Have a Dream!

In some ways, the dream Martin Luther King, Jr., struggled for in 1963 has come true. Today African Americans can be found in every walk of life. They are doctors, nurses, lawyers, teachers, business executives, scientists, astronauts, and more.

Yet, in some ways, the dream remains sadly unfulfilled. Cities remain filled with tension. Too few African Americans sit in the top offices of major corporations. Unacceptable numbers of African American teenagers drop out of school, becoming unemployable. Even today, too many African Americans find their job progress barred by prejudice. The nation still has yet to see an African American President or Vice President.

Another remnant of the past haunting African Americans is poverty. The effects of poverty are poisoning life in the ghettos. Harsh conditions in inner cities have been made worse by violent confrontations with the police. Many African Americans have been subjected to police abuse. Reports have been made complaining about racist remarks, beatings, and unfair arrests.

The most difficult form of discrimination to eliminate is not caused by individuals. The discrimination comes from U.S. **institutions**. Institutions are schools, businesses, hospitals, police forces, and other groups.

Most institutions have rules against discrimination, but the rules are not always obeyed. People who come from a poor neighborhood may find it difficult to get a job with these institutions. Teenagers who grow up in poverty often drop out of school to get low paying jobs. A person who has not graduated from high school or college will not have the same employment opportunities as someone who has.

Much remains to be done before all African Americans achieve Martin Luther King, Jr.'s dream. Still, all Americans can take pride in the achievements of many African Americans today.

Thinking It Over

1. What gains have African Americans made in government?
2. What role does education play in improving job opportunities?

Follow-Up Review

Identifying Main Ideas

1. Why did Martin Luther King, Jr., oppose U.S. participation in the Vietnam War?
2. What accomplishments has the Civil Rights Movement made in voting rights for African Americans?
3. What role did African Americans play in the U.S. effort in Vietnam?

Working Together

Work as a class to organize an exhibit for an "Awareness Day" on the Civil Rights Movement. Then form small groups to create murals, skits, and group discussions. Invite veterans of the Civil Rights Movement to speak to your class on this day.

Active Learning

Asking Questions Review the questions you created while reading the Follow-Up chapter. List your questions and then with a small group of classmates, combine your lists. Choose the ten best questions. Then, with your group, write answers for these questions. Practice interviewing one another within your group. Perform your interviews for the class.

Lessons for Today

The Kerner Commission of 1967 predicted that the United States would become two societies—one black and one white. Do you think that the Kerner Commission's prediction has come true? Is the United States two societies? What evidence is there to support your opinion?

What Might You Have Done?

Imagine that you are preparing a speech to give to a group of civil right's activists. The group has just received the news that Martin Luther King, Jr., has been assasinated. You want your speech to inspire the activists to continue their work for the Civil Right's Movement. What might you say or suggest to inspire the activists to continue their struggle?

GLOSSARY

A

assassin one who murders by surprise attack, especially one who carries out a plot to kill a prominent person

B

Black Power a movement among African Americans beginning in the 1960s emphasizing racial pride and social equality through the creation of political and cultural institutions run by African Americans

boycott to refuse to use or buy the goods or services of a company

C

casualty people who have been killed or injured, especially in war

civil disobedience refusal to obey a law that a person thinks is unjust

civil rights the rights given to U.S. citizens and protected by the Constitution

compromise an agreement that is made by each side giving up some of what they want

convention a meeting of members of a particular group, such as a political party

D

delegate a person who is authorized to act as a representative for another

desegregate to end segregation

discriminate to treat someone in a different way based on their race, religion, or sex

E

exile forced removal from one's country

F

federalize to put under the federal government's control

Freedom Rides a civil rights project that involved protesters riding buses across state lines in the South to test whether those states were allowing illegal segregation on interstate buses

G

ghetto a poor section of a city where a minority or ethnic group lives due to social, economic, or legal pressure

grassroots to work at the local level

H

hustler a small-time crook

I

illiterate the inability to read and write

institution a large organization, such as a school, business, or hospital

integrate to bring together or unify; to open to people of all races or ethnic groups without restriction; to desegregate

interstate involving, existing between, or connecting two or more states

L

literacy the ability to read and write

literacy test a test that measures a person's ability to read and write; a test used before the mid-1960s throughout the South to prevent African Americans from registering to vote

lynching to hang or otherwise murder by mob action for supposed crimes

M

manifesto a statement of beliefs

militant aggressively active in support of a cause

mosque a Muslim house of worship

N

nationalism devotion to a country or group

nonviolence the peaceful refusal to obey unjust laws

P

picket to walk or assemble outside a place to publicize your cause

propoganda the spreading of ideas in order to shape people's opinion

psychology the study of human behavior

poll tax a tax someone must pay in order to vote

R

reconciliation to reestablish a close relationship between two parties

recruit to enroll

register to vote to get one's name on an official list of voters; a U.S. citizen must register before he or she may vote

S

segregation the policy and practice of separating people by race

sharecropper a farmer who works on a plot of land owned by another, paying for it with a share of the crops

sit-in a protest demonstration in which participants sit themselves in an appropriate place and refuse to move until their demands are met

suits court proceeding to recover a right or claim

symbol a word, picture, or thing that stands for something else

T

theology the study of religion

U

unanimous complete agreement

unemployment not having a job

unseat to replace or remove from a location or position, especially to remove from political office

V

volunteer a person who provides a free service

INDEX

Nixon, E.D., *40–41*, *43*, *44*, *45*, *46*
Nonviolence, *42*, *46*, *52*, *53*, *95*, *106*

O

Oklahoma City, sit-ins in, *50*

P

Parks, Raymond, *40*
Parks, Rosa, *7*, *37–40*, *44*, *45*, *46*
Pattillo, Melba, *27–28*, *30*, *33*
Pearson, Levi, *7*, *13*
Philadelphia (Mississippi), murder of civil rights workers, *76*
Picket, *55*
Plessy, Homer A., *5*
Plessy v. *Ferguson*, *5–6*, *13*
Poll tax, *22*
Propaganda, political, *35–36*
Psychological impact of segregation, *16–18*
Public facilities desegregation of, *56–58*, *69*
See also Sit-ins

R

Ray, Gloria, *27*
Reconciliation, *62*
Recruit, *93*, *94*
Register to vote. See Voter registration
Richmond, David, *50*
Riots, *85*, *98*, *108*, *111*
Roberts, Terrance, *27*, *32*
Robinson, Jackie, *10*, *12*
Robinson, Jo Ann, *40*
Rock Hill (South Carolina), Freedom Riders in, *62*
Rustin, Bayard, *62*

S

School desegregation
Brown case, *15–19*
Little Rock resistance to, *24–33*
NAACP and, *13–15*

School segregation, *50*
defenders of, *18*
inequalities in, *12–13*
Levi Pearson's challenge to, *13*
psychological impact of, *16–18*
"separate but equal" policy in, *18*, *22*
Schwerner, Michael, *7*, *75*, *76*, *78*, *83*, *87*
Schwerner, Rita, *83*
SCLC. *See* Southern Christian Leadership Conference
Seale, Bobby, *111*
Segregation
of buses, *38–39*, *62*
Jim Crow laws, *6–7*, *22*
of lunch counters, *51*
Plessy decision, *5–6*, *13*
in public places, *50*, *55*
See also School segregation
"Separate but equal," *18*, *22*
Shabazz, Betty, *99*
Sharecroppers, *9*, *78*
Sit-ins
civil disobedience and, *55–56*
leaders of, *57*
lunch counter, *50–52*, *54*, *55*
nonviolence of, *53*
spread of, *52*, *55*
success of, *56–58*
SNCC. *See* Student Nonviolent Coordinating Committee
Southern Christian Leadership Conference (SCLC), *46*, *56*
Southern Manifesto, *26*
Spirituals, *53*, *55*
Student Nonviolent Coordinating Committee (SNCC), *62*, *85*, *104*
Black power in, *105–106*, *110*, *114*
founding of, *52–53*
leadership change in, *106*, *110*, *114*
See also Freedom Summer
Supreme Court, U.S.
on bus desegregation, *46*

on school desegregation, *18–19*
on segregation, *6*, *13*
Thurgood Marshall on, *20*
Symbol, *93*

T

Theology, *41*
Thomas, Jefferson, *27*, *28*, *32*

U

Unanimous decision, of Supreme Court, *18*
Universal Negro Improvement Association (UNIA), *90–91*
University of Mississippi, *104*
Unseat, *83*

V

Volunteers, in Freedom Summer, *76–77*, *78*
Voter registration, *50*, *58*, *104*
Freedom Summer drives, *76–77*, *82*
Jim Crow laws and, *22*
tactics against, *77–78*, *81–82*
Voting Rights Act of 1965, *108*

W

Walls, Carlotta, *27*
War on Poverty, *85*
Warren, Earl, *18*
Washington, D.C.
March on, *71*, *95*
riots in, *98*
Watts riots, *108*
Wells, Ida B., *8*
"We Shall Overcome," *55*
White backlash, *108*
White Citizens' Councils, *25*
Wichita (Kansas), sit-ins in, *50*
Wilkins, Roy, *105*
Woolworth (F.W.), lunch counter sit-ins at, *50–52*, *55*, *57*
World War II, *10*

ACKNOWLEDGMENTS

Grateful acknowledgment is made to the following publishers, authors, and other copyright holders:

p. 17: From *Removing A Badge Of Slavery: The Record Of Brown V. Board Of Education*, ed. Mark Whitman. NY: Markus Wiener Publishing Company, 1993 pp. 49-51. Used by permission of Marcus Wiener.

p. 29: From *The Long Shadow Of Little Rock*, by Daisy Bates. NY: David McKay, 1962, pp. 73-76. Used by permission of Daisy Bates.

p. 39: From *Rosa Parks: My Story* by Rosa Parks with Jim Haskins. Copyright (c) 1992 by Rosa Parks. Used by permission of Dial Books for Young Readers, a division of Penguin Books USA Inc.

p. 92: From *The Autobiography Of Malcolm X* by Malcolm X and Alex Haley. Copyright (c) 1964 by Alex Haley with Malcolm X. Copyright (c) 1965 by Alex Haley with Betty Shabazz. Reprinted by permission of Random House Inc.

p. 109: Globe Fearon Educational Publisher has executed a reasonable and concerted effort to contact the author of the speech by Stockley Carmichael on July 28, 1966 noted in *Notes & Comment*. Globe Fearon Educational Publisher eagerly invites any persons knowledgeable about the whereabouts of the authors or agents to contact Globe Fearon Educational Publisher to arrange for the customary publishing transactions.

Grateful acknowledgment is made to the following for illustrations, photographs, and reproductions on the pages indicated:

Photo credits: **Cover:** Wide World; Library of Congress; **Title Page:** Wide World; **p.5:** Bob Adelman, Magnum Photos; **p. 6:** ©1995 Danny Lyon, Magnum Photos; **p. 8:** UPI/Bettmann; **p. 10:** National Archives; **p. 11:** Matt Herron/Take Stock; **p. 12:** ©1962 Danny Lyon, Magnum Photos; **p. 15:** Time Life; **p. 16:** ©Joe Cavello, Black Star; **p. 19:** UPI/Bettmann; **p. 20:** UPI/Bettmann; **p. 23:** UPI/Bettmann; **p. 25:** Wide World; **p. 26:** UPI/Bettmann; **p. 28:** UPI/Bettmann; **p. 31:** UPI/Bettmann; **p. 33:** UPI/Bettmann; **p. 37:** ©Flip Schulke, Black Star; **p. 40:** UPI/Bettmann Newsphotos; **p. 41:** UPI/Bettmann Newsphotos; **p. 42:** Henri Cartier Bresson, Magnum; **p. 43:** UPI/Bettmann; **p. 49:** UPI/Bettmann; **p. 51:** UPI/Bettmann Newsphoto; **p. 55:** UPI/Bettmann; **p. 56:** UPI/Bettmann; **p. 57:** UPI/Bettmann; **p. 54:** Fred Blackwell, AP/Wide World Photos; **p. 61:** Bob Adelman, Magnum Photos; **p. 63:** ©Flip Schulke, Black Star; **p. 64:** ©1961 Bruce Davidson, Magnum Photos; **p. 66:** ©1985 Charles Moore, Black Star; **p. 67:** ©Flip Schulke, Black Star; **p. 68:** ©1984 Charles Moore, Black Star; **p. 71:** AP/Wide World; **p. 75:** UPI/Bettmann; **p. 77:** ©Charles Moore, Black Star; **p. 79:** Matt Heron/Take Stock; **p. 81:** ©Bern Keating, Black Star; **p. 83:** UPI/Bettmann; **p. 89:** UPI/Bettmann; **p. 93:** UPI/Bettmann; **p. 95:** UPI/Bettmann Newsphotos; **p. 98:** UPI/Bettmann; **p. 96:** AP/Wide World; **p. 97:** UPI/Bettmann; **p. 103:** ©Flip Schulke, Black Star; **p. 104:** UPI/Bettmann Newsphotos; **p. 106:** UPI/Bettmann; **p. 107:** ©1965 Lou Jacobs Jr., Black Star; **p. 112:** ©Bob Fitch, Black Star; **p. 115:** Bruce Davidson, Magnum; **p. 116:** Costa Manos/Magnum Photos; **p. 118:** UPI/Bettmann; **p. 119:** George Ballis/Take Stock